PUBLICATIONS OF RUSSELL SAGE FOUNDATION

Russell Sage Foundation was established in 1907 by Mrs. Russell Sage for the improvement of social and living conditions in the United States. In carrying out its purpose the Foundation conducts research under the direction of members of the staff or in close collaboration with other institutions, and supports programs designed to develop and demonstrate productive working relations between social scientists and other professional groups. As an integral part of its operations, the Foundation from time to time publishes books or pamphlets resulting from these activities. Publication under the imprint of the Foundation does not necessarily imply agreement by the Foundation, its Trustees, or its staff with the interpretations or conclusions of the authors.

The Prediction of Academic Performance

A Theoretical Analysis and Review of Research

David E. Lavin

Department of Sociology
University of Pennsylvania

Russell Sage Foundation · New York · 1965

© 1965
RUSSELL SAGE FOUNDATION
Printed in the United States
of America

*Library of Congress
Catalog Card Number:* 65–19043

CONNECTICUT PRINTERS, INC.
HARTFORD, CONN.

Acknowledgments

In 1958, while at Russell Sage Foundation, I conducted an evaluative survey of recent literature on the determinants of academic achievement. The present volume represents an extension and amplification of an informal report on that survey submitted to the Foundation in 1959. Although the ultimate responsibility for the quality of this volume rests only with me, the final product has benefited from the contributions of several people to whom I wish to express gratitude.

Orville G. Brim, Jr., has been the person most closely associated with this work. He first encouraged me to develop and expand the original report and patiently read each revision, providing incisive and constructive criticism.

David C. Glass and David A. Goslin read earlier drafts, and their comments have contributed to the final product. I am also grateful to Norman Kaplan and Harold J. Bershady for their counsel regarding portions of the manuscript.

In the initial stage of this study, discussions with Norman O. Frederiksen and other staff members at Educational Testing Service acquainted me with relevant work in which they were engaged. I am particularly appreciative of their help.

The heavy task of reviewing several hundred studies was lightened considerably by the substantial assistance provided by Mrs. Zelda F. Gamson. For their diligence and patience in typing various drafts of the manuscript, I am indebted to Miss Eva Reiff, Mrs. Janet Kravitz, and Mrs. Ursula Varano.

DAVID E. LAVIN

Contents

5

Tables, Charts, and Figure

Chapter 1

Introduction

CONCERN WITH THE PREDICTION of academic performance has increased during recent years. One reason for this is the much-publicized growth in the student population. On the college level the increase has outstripped the expansion of facilities, consequently heightening the competition for admission, especially at the better universities and colleges. For college admissions officers the selection of students is more difficult than ever before because the increase in the sheer number of applicants is paralleled by growth in the number of highly qualified candidates. Thus, the responsibility of colleges to be as certain as possible that the students they select will do better than those they exclude is becoming increasingly difficult to fulfill.

A second source of interest in the prediction of academic performance is the growth of programs designed to identify and support the training of students with outstanding talents. Such programs (for example, that of the National Merit Scholarship Corporation) reflect the exigencies of the post-Sputnik Cold War competition and the national need to find those persons able to absorb and use high-level scientific and technical training. If students selected for support by these programs do not perform according to expectations, money is wasted and others who might be better risks are lost to the nation's pool of trained manpower.

A third reason for increased interest in predicting academic performance is the development within the social sciences of the serious, concerted study of education. While long an active concern of psychology, education has not until recently been of equal interest to sociology. Recent developments suggest that education is being given increasing attention by sociology. This is probably because the classroom furnishes a testing ground for basic theory and because sociology is now in a position to provide some answers for the practical problems of education. In 1960 a section on the sociology of education was established in the American Sociological Association, and the *Journal of Educational Sociology* was subsequently made an official publication of the Association.

These developments, along with increased financial support by federal and private agencies, make it likely that the volume of research on education will continue to grow. As part of this growth, it is to be expected that social scientists will contribute increasingly to research on the prediction of academic performance.

Early research on this subject focused primarily on intellective and ability factors as predictors. Recently there have been important shifts in emphasis and in the conceptualization of the problem due to the gradual recognition that some students perform better and some perform worse than predicted by ability tests. The search for causes of these variations in academic performance led first to the consideration of "nonintellective," or personality characteristics. Even more recently the search has led to recognition that the interaction between aspects of the student's personality and his social environment (for example, the characteristics of his school or college) is important.

With new trends and emphases developing, it seems timely that some stock-taking be done.[1] Accordingly, the purpose of this volume is, first, to review recent research on the prediction of academic performance by summarizing what is known about the role of intellective factors, the personality characteristics, and the social settings that are related to performance. Second, it evaluates each approach in terms of a number of theoretical and methodological issues and indicates some of the directions subsequent research might take.

Of the nearly 300 sources covered in this review, almost all were published during the period 1953 through 1961, though a few items appearing before 1953 are mentioned to provide continuity with earlier research. While it is true that a three-year gap exists between the cut-off date of the survey of the literature and the publication of this volume, the findings published in the interim would not alter the conclusions of this book.[2] The types of studies to be included are limited. Research on the relation between educational techniques (for example, large vs. small classes, programed learning vs. traditional methods) and academic performance was not included. Studies of specialized populations, such as technical high schools, medical schools, schools in foreign countries, and so on were not included unless they introduced a promising technique or variable that could be applied to studies of broader populations. On the other hand, a few studies not explicitly concerned with academic performance have been included because they are potentially relevant to this problem. While this review is not a complete enumeration of relevant research, within the limits set, it omits, to our knowledge, no major study.

This volume covers six major topics. Chapter 2 deals with the meaning of the concept of academic performance and problems of its measurement. Chapter 3 discusses several theoretical and methodological problems pertaining to the prediction of achievement.

Research emphasizing intellectual characteristics is reviewed in Chapter 4. Chapter 5 concerns the findings of studies that assess the relation between a student's nonintellective, personality characteristics and his academic performance. Chapter 6 reviews sociological research—that is, studies concerned with the ways in which characteristics of the social environment produce variations in academic performance.

Chapter 7 sets forth those studies that use, primarily, a social structure and personality approach to analyze the interaction between characteristics of the person and characteristics of the social setting as they combine to influence academic performance. With these few studies as examples, the directions for future research are stated and an illustrative research design is presented.

VALUE JUDGMENTS IN THE CHOICE
OF PERFORMANCE CRITERIA

In studies of academic achievement the traditional criterion of performance is the student's grades. Other criteria are occasionally used either in addition to or in place of the traditional approach. For example, some researchers have been interested in predicting whether students will graduate from college.[3] Others have been concerned with criteria such as intellectual curiosity,[4] acceptance in graduate school,[5] long-range career success of good and poor students,[6] and the quality of verbal expression of graduate students.[7] Despite the occasional use of these criteria, in the overwhelming number of cases, student grades are the sole index of performance.

The overriding use of this criterion has been a cause of concern to some persons.[8] There are three issues here. The first involves the question of the goals and value premises that underlie the heavy emphasis on grades as an index of academic performance. A second is whether there are other socially significant values and goals in terms of which aspects of performance besides grades become important. Third is the question of the degree to which the traditional emphasis on academic performance is related to these other values.

From the standpoint of the admissions officers of colleges and graduate schools, the value of the traditional criterion, grades, is clear, since to them it is of practical importance to screen out candidates who would be unable to complete successfully a program of study leading to a degree. The emphasis on grades for admission to college also causes the high schools to stress their importance. Because of such practical considerations and perhaps because of the ease of obtaining data on grades, high grades have assumed the status of a terminal value; academic performance, particularly as represented by high levels of academic achievement, has become an end in itself.

However, if we view the educational process within a broader context, other aspects of the student role may assume greater importance. Formal education is one aspect of the socialization process. When we speak of this process, we imply that we are socializing *for* something—primarily for performance in a variety of adult roles. Considered in this way, an important feature of the student role is its transitional character. This characteristic leads to the question of how various characteristics of performance in the student role are related to performance in future adult roles. Thus, if we ask about the relationship between scholarship and later occupational success or an inquiring, critical attitude of mind or creativity, we can see that high academic performance per se may not always be meaningful. To put it another way, if career success, critical-mindedness, and creativity are valuable for a variety of personal and societal goals, what is the meaning of grades (especially the implicit value position that *high* grades are inherently good) in the context of these other values? In short, there is a question as to why—and for what—grades are important.

A few examples will illuminate this point. Frequently college-educated women who marry and devote all their time to their families feel that much of what they do is meaningless, dull, and unsatisfying—even if they experience no conflict between commitment to family life and the desire for a career. Some women, on the other hand, may not experience this dissatisfaction because they pursue intellectual interests acquired during college, thus maintaining a degree of stimulation even within the home context.

We assume that any college participating in the education of women would believe that the education, even of those who will be totally committed to running a home, should not simply end with the granting of a diploma. On the contrary, most colleges would hope that the students, in addition to learning sheer content, will acquire an enduring attitude of intellectual curiosity. However, even though the acquisition of such an attitude may be viewed as desirable, not all college women develop it. Who are the women capable of becoming intellectually curious? What distinguishes them from women who will not develop such an attitude? Are some college environments conducive to this development for certain types of women but not for others? Can it be assumed that women who obtain high grades in college are, by definition, more intellectually curious than women whose performance is not so high? These are unanswered questions. If colleges are interested in producing intellectual curiosity, they may have to pay attention to more than grades. Indeed, concern with the development of intellectual curiosity might involve modification of the traditional criteria for admission to college.

A second example has to do with the extent to which grades are related to outstanding occupational performance. Are the more eminent American physicists, or architects, or business executives, or psychologists uniformly individuals whose college performance, as indexed by grades, was exemplary? Some evidence suggests that with respect to creativity this is not the case. MacKinnon,[9] for example, points out that studies of creative research scientists and architects indicate that they often did not have outstanding grades in college, and many compiled records that were actually quite mediocre. Similarly, Holland,[10] in a study of the correlates of college grades, makes the point that for highly intelligent students those factors predictive of high performance tend also to be negatively related to creativity. This suggests that high grades alone are not a useful index for identifying those who will make creative contributions after college.

If grades will not predict future eminence, and if the early identification of outstanding talent is a task worth pursuing, there is a need to develop additional criteria of good student performance. In short, as soon as education is considered in the context of certain societal values and needs, it is evident that in addition to grades, other dimensions of student behavior need to be considered.

Of course, grades are not unimportant. They are unquestionably an index of competence in school work, but within the context of some personal and societal goals, reliance upon grades as the *only* criterion of student performance is unwarranted.

While the considerations discussed above are important and

deserve the attention of future research, it is not the concern of this volume to develop additional criteria of performance in the student role; rather, it is to review and evaluate the existing research, which defines performance mainly in terms of grades.

NOTES TO CHAPTER 1

1. For a review of work on the college level see Stein, Morris I., *Personality in College Admissions,* College Entrance Examination Board, New York, 1963.

2. Much of the most recent work is concerned with the social environment of the school and its relations to personality and values. A good sample of this work may be seen in the *School Review,* vol. 71, no. 3, 1963.

3. Boyer, Roscoe A., "A Study of the Academic Success of Undergraduate Students as Identified by Aptitude Test Profiles," *Dissertation Abstracts,* vol. 17, 1958, pp. 89–90; French, John W., "Validation of New Item Types Against Four-Year Academic Criteria," *Journal of Educational Psychology,* vol. 49, 1958, pp. 67–76; Worrell, Leonard, "Level of Aspiration and Academic Success," *Journal of Educational Psychology,* vol. 50, 1959, pp. 47–54.

4. Brown, Donald R., "Non-Intellective Qualities and the Perception of the Ideal Student by College Faculty," *Journal of Educational Sociology,* vol. 33, 1960, pp. 269–278.

5. Buckton, LaVerne, and Jerome E. Doppelt, "Freshman Tests as Predictors of Scores on Graduate and Professional School Examinations," *Journal of Counseling Psychology,* vol. 2, 1955, pp. 146–149; Melton, Richard S., "Differentiation of Successful and Unsuccessful Premedical Students," *Journal of Applied Psychology,* vol. 38, 1955, pp. 397–400.

6. Walker, John L., "Counselors' Judgments in the Prediction of the Occupational and Educational Performance of Former High School Students," *Journal of Educational Research,* vol. 49, 1955, pp. 81–91.

7. Webb, Sam C., "Differential Prediction of Success in a Graduate School," *Journal of Educational Research,* vol. 50, 1956, pp. 45–54.

8. Fishman, Joshua A., "Unsolved Criterion Problems in the Selection of College Students," *Harvard Educational Review,* vol. 28, 1958, pp. 340–349; Dyer, Henry S., "The Past, Present, and Future of Admissions Research," *College Board Review,* no. 42, 1960, pp. 21–25.

9. MacKinnon, D. W., "What Do We Mean by Talent and How Do We Test for It?" in *The Search for Talent.* College Entrance Examination Board, New York, 1960, pp. 20–29.

10. Holland, John L., "The Prediction of College Grades from Personality and Aptitude Variables," *Journal of Educational Psychology,* vol. 51, 1960, pp. 245–254.

Chapter 2

Academic Performance: The Meaning of the Concept and Problems of Its Measurement

BECAUSE OF THE COMPLEXITY and extensiveness of the survey of the literature presented in Chapters 4 to 7, there is a danger that the reader may become overwhelmed by the findings and thus lose a sense of the general conclusions and the directions for further research suggested by an evaluation of them. Therefore, a context for discussing the findings is provided in this chapter and the next. The present chapter examines the meaning of the concept of academic performance and considers several theoretical and methodological problems of its measurement.

As traditionally used, the term "academic performance" refers to some method of expressing a student's scholastic standing. Usually this is a grade for a course, an average for a group of courses in a subject area, or an average for all courses expressed on a 0-to-100 or other quantitative scale. Often, particularly on the college level, the grade is first expressed nominally (A, B, C) and is then converted to a numerical value (such as A = 4, B = 3, and so forth), so that a grade-point average for all courses can be computed. The grade-point average is then taken as the measure of academic performance. On the elementary school level, performance is often evaluated on a verbal scale ranging from "excellent" to "poor." Another measure of performance sometimes used instead of grades is the standardized achievement test.[1]

18

COMPARABILITY OF GRADES AS INDICATORS
OF PERFORMANCE

A major aim of the studies reviewed in this volume is to discover those factors that will enable us to predict academic performance. This search for predictive factors has focused primarily upon various characteristics of the student, such as his aptitudes, his personality traits, and the like. Relationships between such predictors and performance criteria are not very strong. Researchers usually view this as an indication of: (1) failure to isolate enough of the right variables, and/or (2) measurement error in the predictors. Relatively little attention is given to the possibility that low correlations might also be due to uncontrolled sources of variation in grades themselves. Although this problem has been discussed,[2] it has not been investigated systematically. When one examines this question, it becomes clear that there are so many sources of uncontrolled variation that substantial increases in predictability may not be forthcoming until they are controlled.

These sources of variation fall into two categories. First, not all students take the same courses. They major in different curricular areas (particularly on the college level), and some types of majors may be more difficult than others.

Second, teachers use different criteria in assigning grades. Consider for a moment what is involved here. First, there are the examinations themselves; these may be objective, or of the essay type, or a combination of the two. In addition, oral participation in class sometimes is important, and other times not. Third, whether or not term papers are assigned is variable, and the weight they receive in determining a grade also varies. Since not all students have the same instructors, and since instructors vary in terms of the criteria they use, as well as in the importance they assign to each criterion, it is clear that there is also considerable uncontrolled variation here. Moreover, students differ in their ability to perform well in different areas; some may express themselves better in writing than orally, and some perform better on essay than on objective examinations. In addition, there is the question of whether some teachers are "harder" markers than others. Furthermore, some evidence suggests that implicit, subjective criteria are involved in teachers' grading practices.[3] We refer here to the possibility that certain characteristics of the student, such as his sex and social class background, affect the quality of the relationship between the student and the teacher. The nature of this social relationship may, in turn, partly determine the grade the student receives.

Very little effort has been devoted to controlling these sources of variation. Because of this, student grades lack a high degree of comparability. An analogy will illustrate the problem. Let us assume that we administer an intelligence test under several conditions: to some persons alone; to others in a group; and to still others under conditions of emotional stress. Let us also assume that we are subsequently ignorant of the condition under which any given individual was tested. In these circumstances, two scores of equal numerical value would not necessarily indicate equal ability, and two scores of greatly unequal numerical value could quite possibly be obtained by two persons of equivalent ability. In short, we would have made only a crude ordering of the persons' intelligence. We might be on fairly safe ground in asserting that the subject with the very highest score was brighter than the person with the lowest score, but aside from the extremes, we could have little confidence that the ordering of scores was valid. If we used these scores to predict performance on some kind of task, it certainly would not be surprising to find that the correlation of intelligence and task performance was very low. This would be due largely to the uncontrolled sources of variation in the measurement of intelligence.

Academic performance, as indexed by the grade-point average, is subject to analogous difficulties. In any distribution of grade-point averages, some have been obtained by students concentrating in physics, others by students majoring in history, still others by those in physical education, and so forth. There is a question as to whether it is meaningful to compare averages of students across majors. It would be more appropriate to study the determinants of performance within curricular groupings. Failure to do this is one reason for our inability to predict performance with any great degree of precision. In fact, considering the effects of all the factors that determine grades and yet are not controlled, one wonders how it is possible to predict them with even the fair degree of success already attained.

As noted at the beginning of this discussion, the problem of controls with regard to grades has not been totally neglected. Fishman suggests the use of uniform tests (such as standard achievement tests) as one means of overcoming the error associated with the use of grades as an index of academic performance.[4] Like the grade-point average, however, this alternative does not, in itself, provide a control on the different course distributions taken by students. However, it would help to eliminate uncontrolled subjective criteria that may enter into the teachers' grading practices. For this reason it would seem advisable to use uniform test scores as supplementary criteria of performance. However, their use as the sole criteria of performance is questionable because it would lead away from a consideration of the teacher as a theoretically significant factor. That is, subjective factors in grading practices should not be viewed simply as "error" to be avoided by the substitution of other criteria of performance. To do this would not enhance our understanding of the determinants of grades. Let us examine this matter further.

A student's grade is more than something that characterizes him as does his score on a personality inventory or an intelligence test; that is, it is not simply a personal characteristic or a trait. Rather, a grade should be viewed as a function of the interaction between student and teacher. In short, it is one index of this social relationship. So considered, it is clear that if we want to predict a grade, we must know something not only about the student (his ability, his personality, his values), but about the teacher as well.

We could pose the issue not as a matter of predicting the academic performance of students, but as a question predicting the grading behavior of teachers. For example, one might study the effects of the sex of the student upon the "objectivity" of the particular teacher's grading practices. One study considered this topic and found that the objectivity of male teachers is influenced by the sex of the student.[5]

Research directed toward the measurement and control of sources of variation in grades is needed. Some aspects of such research will be more difficult than others. Thus, it is a relatively straightforward matter to separate students according to the curricular area of concentration, since these data are easily obtainable from school records. On the other hand, the study of subjective factors in teachers' grading practices poses more difficulties, because these are harder to define and to measure reliably. Nevertheless, attention to these problems should enhance our ability to predict academic performance and enrich our theoretical understanding of it.

PERFORMANCE GROUPINGS AND THE CONTROL OF ABILITY

As we shall see in Chapter 4, the relationship between ability and academic performance is well documented, and the great majority of studies are no longer concerned primarily with demonstrating this finding. Rather, they attempt to improve predictions through the use of additional factors of a nonintellective nature. In research of this kind it is important to ensure that the nonintellective variables are independent of ability. Failure to do this creates serious problems in the interpretation of findings. An example will help to illustrate this problem.

Suppose it is found that a positive self-image (high self-esteem) is positively correlated with school grades. That is, the higher one's self-esteem, the higher one's grades are likely to be. Does this necessarily mean that self-esteem is an independent predictor of school performance? The answer is that this is not necessarily the case, because we might find that self-esteem was also positively correlated with ability. If this were true, it could be argued that both school performance and self-esteem are partly determined by ability. In this case we could say that self-esteem is an indirect index of ability level. Thus, self-esteem could not be considered an independent predictor of school performance. In short, one cannot assess the usefulness of nonintellective factors unless they are independent of ability.

Essentially, there are two approaches used to control for ability. The first involves the use of partial correlation techniques;[6] the second, the selection of students equated for ability but differing in grades. Thus, by the second method, one obtains groupings of students into different performance levels, but no group differs from any other group in ability. The strategy is then to assess whether these groups differ on some factor such as a personality characteristic. In this way the personality determinants of academic performance may be discovered. These two methods of analysis represent simply two different ways of dealing with the same problem. That is, if a personality variable is positively correlated with academic performance or if it distinguishes between achievement groupings, positive findings lead to the same conclusion (when ability is controlled); namely, that the personality variable under consideration is useful in accounting for variation in academic performance.

Studies using the second approach often fail to ensure that the performance groupings are actually comparable with regard to ability, however, because they use incorrect procedures for composing the groups. Thus, it is important to examine these procedures.

High and Low Achievement

One procedure yields performance groups designated as high and low achievers. These terms refer to absolute levels of performance. For example, one might decide to define high achievement as the attainment of at least an A average and low achievement as the attainment of no higher than a D average. Of course, if one were then to compare the high and low achievers on some personality characteristic, there would be no way of assuring that the latter was independent of ability. In order to assure that ability is controlled, either of two procedures could be used. First, one might start with a sample that is homogeneous as to ability—for example, a sample of gifted (high IQ) children. Within this group some might be high achievers, and others, low achievers. The two groups may then be compared on nonintellective factors, and ability is controlled.

A second method involves the assignment of students to high- and low-achieving groups on the basis of their grades. Students are then matched for ability. That is, a low achiever with an IQ of, say, 115 is paired with a high achiever of the same IQ, a low achiever of 105 IQ is matched with a high-achieving counterpart, and so on.[7] This procedure assures that there will be no difference in average IQ between the high- and low-achieving groups. One difference between this procedure and the first one should be noted. In the first method, the high and low achievers are homogeneous with regard to ability (in the illustration they are all of high intelligence). However, in the second method the two groups do not differ in their average ability, but they are not necessarily homogeneous in ability. That is, within each group there will be some students of high ability, some of medium, and some of low ability. While both of these methods control for ability, the distinction between them is of theoretical importance. However, because this point is also relevant for other methods of defining performance groupings, further discussion is deferred to a later part of this chapter.

Overachievement and Underachievement

As is well known, the performance of some students exceeds the level that would be predicted from measures of intellectual ability, while the performance of others falls below the predicted level. The first type of student is known as the overachiever, and the second, the underachiever.

It is incorrect to consider high and low achievement to be synonymous with over- and underachievement. The distinction between the concepts is that high and low achievement are defined in terms of an absolute standard of performance, while over- and underachievement involve the discrepancy between predicted and actual performance. If high achievement is defined as the attainment of at least an A average and low achievement as the attainment of no higher than a low C average, then a student could be a high achiever but not an overachiever, or he could be an overachiever but not a high achiever. An example of the former would be a student of very high ability who attains an A average. If his grades are at a level predicted for a person of his talent, he would not be an overachiever, even though his level of performance is high. On the other hand, if a student of very limited ability attained a B average, his performance might exceed the level predicted on the basis of ability. Thus, he would be an overachiever, but not a high achiever.

Studies of over- and underachievement are found very frequently in the literature. However, the choice of terms seems unfortunate. For one reason, such labels tend to raise intelligence and aptitude tests to an almost sacrosanct level. That is, since over- and underachievement are defined as departures from what ability measures would lead us to expect, there is a tendency to think that these departures are somehow mysterious and inexplicable—that somehow the intelligence or aptitude test just cannot be wrong. It would be more accurate to say that for the prediction of academic performance, ability is but one kind of necessary information. From this point of view, what is left after ability has been used as a predictor is not over- and underachievement, but unexplained variation, much of which may be accounted for by other predictive factors. In short, these terms actually refer to the inaccuracy involved in predicting academic performance from ability measures alone. If this is not recognized, we may fail to look for other significant classes of predictors.

A second reason that the choice of terms is unfortunate is that they have acquired negative connotations, arousing in some the idea that the overachiever is a "grind" who lacks such desirable qualities as sociability, "well-roundedness," and the like. On the other hand, the underachiever may be thought of as one who is lazy, undisciplined, and immature. In this volume such connotations are not intended.

In spite of these shortcomings, the terms are currently used in the educational field. For this reason they are used here, with the hope that the reader will keep in mind the limitations described above.

In addition to the fact that these terms often have misleading connotations, deficiencies in the operational procedures for obtaining over- and underachieving groups are found in many studies. These deficiencies result in a failure to control effectively for ability. For this reason it is well to consider the procedures used.

In some studies, over- and underachieving groups are defined by pairing students. That is, students are matched for ability but are widely different in grades. For example, if two students each had an observed IQ of 115, but one had an A average and the other a C average, the first might be designated the overachiever and the second, the underachiever. This technique does control for ability. However, it is not consistent with the conceptual definition of overachievement and underachievement, since these terms refer to a discrepancy between predicted performance and actual performance. For this reason, high achievement and low achievement are more appropriate labels for the groups isolated by this technique.

A second procedure for isolating achievement groups is based on percentile discrepancies between ability and academic performance. For example, if a student's aptitude score places him in a percentile that is higher than his percentile for grades, he is designated an underachiever. Conversely, if his ability percentile is lower than his percentile for grades, he is designated an overachiever. A third method of grouping consists of calculating a ratio between scholastic performance and ability. For example, one could divide the grade-point average by the ability measure. In this case, overachievers would be characterized by higher ratios than underachievers. However, an arbitrary decision must be made concerning the minimum and maximum magnitudes that will be used in forming the groups.

Both the second and third methods discussed exhibit a weakness that is often overlooked. This difficulty concerns what is called the "regression effect,"[8] which refers to the likelihood that for any set of observations on individuals, such as their scores on aptitude and their school grades, an extreme score on one measure tends to be associated with a less extreme score on the second measure. The explanation of this phenomenon is as follows: Observed scores are determined by two factors, the true score and measurement error. The sum of these factors is the obtained score. We assume that measurement error is random—that no systematic factor influencing the error in a particular direction is involved. Thus, if a person scores high on one measure, this will be due in part to the error component. However, if error is random, this component is not likely to influence his score in the same direction on the second measure. Consequently, he will tend to be less extreme on the second score. Applied to the question of academic achievement, this would mean that a student who obtained a very high aptitude score would probably be less extreme on a measure of achievement such as school grades. For example, if a student was in the ninety-fifth percentile on aptitude, his academic achievement percentile would probably be somewhat lower. This is because his high rank on aptitude may be due in part to measurement error. In short, his "real" score on the aptitude test is probably somewhat lower than his obtained score. Thus, it would be erroneous to classify this student as an underachiever. Yet many studies commit this error.

The effects of this error are demonstrated in Chart 1 on page 28, which presents relationships between observed ability and observed school grades. It can be seen that for those of high measured ability, overachievement cannot occur; while for those of low measured ability, underachievement cannot occur. That is, the academic performance category of a student in the highest ability grouping can only be equal to or less than the ability classification; therefore he cannot be an overachiever. On the other hand, the performance of a student in the lowest ability group can only be equal to or greater than the ability classification; therefore he cannot be an underachiever. Thus, it is to be expected that students of very high ability will be overrepresented in the underachiever group, and that those of very low ability will be overrepresented among the overachievers. Consequently, the two groups will not be equivalent in ability. In such cases, it would be impossible to assess the role of a personality factor in differentiating over- and underachievers, because ability has, in effect, not been controlled.

CHART 1. TYPES OF SCHOLASTIC PERFORMANCE AT
DIFFERENT ABILITY LEVELS

Observed ability	Observed school grades		
	Low	Medium	High
High	Pronounced underachievement	Underachievement	Performance equal to capacity
Medium	Underachievement	Performance equal to capacity	Overachievement
Low	Performance equal to capacity	Overachievement	Pronounced overachievement

This failure to control for ability occurs wherever the method for picking achievement groups focuses on the discrepancy between *observed* aptitude and *observed* school grades. The solution to this problem lies in operationally defining overachievement and underachievement as discrepancies between observed grades and *predicted* grades. In this case, the predicted grade is a value computed from a regression equation between aptitude and obtained grades. Using this technique, the overachiever would be the student whose actual grade exceeds his predicted grade, and the underachiever would be the student whose actual grade is lower than his predicted grade.[9] This procedure for constituting groups controls for ability. Figure 1, which presents the relationship between ability and grades, illustrates this. For purposes of simplicity, the usual grouping assumes three kinds of ability: low, medium, and high. The straight line labeled "Predicted grade" is called the regression line. The slope of this line expresses the degree of correlation between ability and grades. That is, it shows the average increase in obtained grades corresponding to increases in ability scores.[10] It can be seen that it is possible for

FIGURE 1. CORRELATION OF ABILITY SCORES AND OBTAINED GRADES

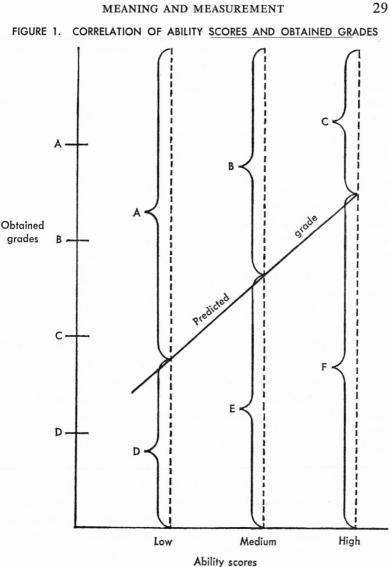

those of low ability to obtain grades that are lower than predicted. Conversely, it is possible for those of high ability to obtain grades that are higher than predicted. In short, the achievement level of students who are at the extremes on aptitude is not restricted as in Chart 1.

PERFORMANCE AT DIFFERENT ABILITY LEVELS

Failure to equate performance groups for ability is not the only shortcoming of many studies. Another difficulty is that both high and low achievement and over- and underachievement may not be unitary phenomena. For example, there may be not one, but several *types* of over- and underachievement. By "type" we mean to distinguish between the overachiever who is high on ability and the overachiever who is low on ability. Thus, the accompanying figure shows that there are, theoretically, three types of overachievement corresponding to the three levels of ability. These are designated by the A, B, and C sections of the vertical broken lines. These broken lines indicate possible obtained grades at each ability level. The D, E, and F sections of the broken lines designate three types of underachievement—that is, high-, medium-, and low-ability underachievers.

Given these possibilities, we suggest that the factors responsible for underachievement at high levels of ability may be different or operate differently from those causing underachievement at medium or low levels of ability. It is important to make provision in research for analyzing these possibilities. Otherwise relationships may be obscured and the researcher may come to the conclusion that a given variable is not predictive of over- and underachievement when, in fact, it may predict at some ability levels, but not at others. For example, suppose that a variable such as "test-taking anxiety" is negatively related to underachievement for low-aptitude students. That is, the higher the anxiety level in examination situations, the lower the performance on the examination. Furthermore, suppose that for high-aptitude underachievers, no such relationship exists, perhaps because very few high-aptitude students are high on test anxiety, or perhaps because at this level of aptitude, such anxiety does not have negative effects on performance. Failure to analyze academic performance within these different ability levels might obscure any relationship between test anxiety and performance. At present, very few studies take this into account.[11]

THE AVERAGE ACHIEVER

A final consideration concerns those students whose actual performance is not extreme. In studies of high and low achievement these are the students whose performance falls between the high and low groups. In studies of over- and underachievement they are the students whose actual performance corresponds closely to predicted performance.

Because of the emphasis on studying the extreme groups, these "average achievers" have often been neglected. When only the extreme groups are considered, the researcher is, in effect, assuming a linear relation between some predictor variable and academic performance. However, if the extremes do not differ on the predictor variable, the possibility of a curvilinear relationship cannot be considered unless the third group, the average achievers, has been included in the sample. For example, suppose that both over- and underachievers are equally low on a variable such as "self-esteem"—that both have an unfavorable opinion of themselves. If this were the case, we would conclude that self-esteem is unrelated to academic performance. However, it might be that for the average achievers the level of self-esteem is high. In this case the relation of this variable to performance is curvilinear, but we could not discover this if we compared only the over- and underachievers. For this reason, it seems advisable to study the entire range of academic performance.

SUMMARY

This chapter has discussed a number of questions regarding the definition and measurement of academic performance. We have pointed out that there is much uncontrolled variation in performance criteria. Research is hindered because the grades of different students are often not comparable.

Furthermore, there are often deficiencies in the operational definitions of the performance criteria. The result is that performance groups (high and low achievers, under- and overachievers) are not equated for intellectual ability.

The question of analyzing academic performance within different ability levels was discussed. Failure to examine performance within ability levels may sometimes mask the operation of predictive factors that are related to performance in different ways, depending on the ability level.

Finally, the question of the average achiever was examined. It was pointed out that when only the extreme groups (high and low achievers, under- and overachievers) are studied, the presence of curvilinear relationships may be overlooked.

NOTES TO CHAPTER 2

1. Examples are to be found in: Educational Testing Service, *1957 Catalogue of Cooperative Tests,* Princeton, N.J., 1957.

2. Baker, Robert L., and Roy P. Doyle, "Teacher Knowledge of Pupil Data and Marking Practices at the Elementary School Level," *Personnel and Guidance Journal,* vol. 37, 1959, pp. 644–647; Bendig, Albert W., "The Reliability of Letter Grades," *Educational and Psychological Measurement,* vol. 13, 1953, pp. 311–321; Fishman, Joshua A., "Unsolved Criterion Problems in the Selection of College Students," *Harvard Educational Review,* vol. 28, 1958, pp. 340–349; Kelly, Eldon G., "A Study of Consistent Discrepancies Between Instructor Grades and Term-End Examination Grades," *Journal of Educational Psychology,* vol. 49, 1958, pp. 328–334.

3. Data pertaining to this question are presented in Chapter 6.

4. Fishman, Joshua A., *op. cit.*

5. Carter, Robert S., "Non-Intellectual Variables Involved in Teachers' Marks," *Journal of Educational Research,* vol. 47, 1953, pp. 81–95.

6. For a discussion of partial correlation techniques see Guilford, J. P., *Fundamental Statistics in Psychology and Education,* 3d ed., McGraw-Hill Book Co., New York, 1956, chap. 13.

7. A question arises here as to what exactly is meant by the term "matching." If the IQ or aptitude scores are matched only when they are of exactly the same numerical value, this often will cause a large number of cases to be discarded. To overcome this problem, the distribution of ability scores can be grouped into intervals, and any scores falling within a specific interval may be considered to be "matched."

8. For a more extended discussion of the regression effect in relation to studies of academic performance, see Thorndike, Robert L., *The Concepts of Over- and Underachievement,* Bureau of Publications, Teachers College, Columbia University, New York, 1963, pp. 1–15.

9. It should be noted that this technique does involve one unresolved question; namely, how large a discrepancy must exist before a student is classified as an over- or underachiever? The question is important because

in any distribution of actual grades, very few will correspond *exactly* to the predicted grade. Thus, in research a decision must be made specifying the size of the discrepancy that is necessary for classifying students into achievement groups.

10. For a good basic discussion of correlation analysis and related issues, see Guilford, J. P., *op. cit.,* chaps. 8, 15, and 17.

11. Those that do take ability level into account include Horrall, Bernice M., "Academic Performance and Personality Adjustment of Highly Intelligent College Students," *Genetic Psychology Monographs,* vol. 55, 1957, pp. 3–83; Jensen, Vern H., "Influence of Personality Traits on Academic Success," *Personnel and Guidance Journal,* vol. 36, 1958, pp. 497–500.

Chapter 3

Academic Performance: The Problems of Its Prediction

C HAPTER 2 considered problems in the definition of the criterion, academic performance. This chapter deals with a number of methodological difficulties of its prediction. The first section considers problems pertaining to the variables used for prediction. The second section deals with the interpretation of relationships between predictors and performance. And last to be considered are the problems of the general characteristics of study designs.

THE PREDICTORS OF ACADEMIC PERFORMANCE

With regard to the predictors of academic performance, there are at least two important problems that have not received sufficient attention. First, many predictors that have similar labels may, in fact, be measuring different content. That is, poor standardization characterizes much research on predictors. The second difficulty is the obverse of this: some predictive factors that are defined differently on the conceptual level may not actually be independent of one another. These problems are now examined in more detail.

The Standardization of Predictor Measures

A basic end in any area of scientific research is the cumulation of a body of reliable knowledge. However, before a particular fact or empirical relationship can be viewed as established with a high degree of reliability, repeated observations are necessary and rather consistent findings must emerge. Moreover, when investigators are attempting to replicate one another's work, they must be sure that the replication is comparable to the earlier investigation. By comparability, we mean that the operations or procedures of one study should resemble as closely as possible the operations of the other. If this is not the case, obtained discrepancies in findings might be due to the fact that different procedures were used. In short, if procedures are not comparable, the interpretation of differences between studies becomes ambiguous, and this, in turn, hinders the cumulation of knowledge.

This problem is particularly relevant to the assessment of current knowledge about the correlates of academic performance. Many instruments that have similar labels and purportedly measure the same phenomenon are composed of different kinds of items and often involve very different techniques of administration. For example, "achievement motivation" is a predictive factor currently in rather wide use. However, it is the case that achievement motivation is measured in a number of different ways. Sometimes it is measured through the use of projective tests in which the subject is asked to compose a story in response to a picture presented to him. The story is then scored for the frequency with which achievement themes are observed. Achievement motivation is also measured through the use of nonprojective questionnaires. Although the format of such questionnaires may vary, a typical case would involve a series of statements concerning the desire to achieve at a high level in school. The subject might then be asked to indicate the extent to which each statement reflects his own desires.

Suppose now that one study using the projective method and another study using the questionnaire method obtain different findings. For example, the first study might find that when aptitude is controlled, high achievement motivation is associated with higher levels of academic performance; while the second study might find no relationship between motivation and performance. Given this situation, it would be difficult to know whether the discrepancy in findings was due to the use of different measures of motivation or to some other factor. Much of the present inconsistency in findings may be due to the possibility that measures with similar conceptual labels are really dissimilar.

This problem, which characterizes many studies on the prediction of academic performance, hinders our ability to judge the usefulness of various predictive factors. Clearly, what is needed is greater standardization in the use of predictor measures. At least two related steps can be taken in this direction. The first is the initiation of research that is explicitly directed toward the mapping of relationships between alternative measures of the same variable. Once the relations between these measures have been determined, we will be in a better position to compare the findings of studies using them. A second step involves the assessment of the comparative usefulness of alternative measures. That is, studies are needed that will take several of these measures, observe the association of each with academic performance in the same study population, and compare the magnitudes of these associations. In this way the poorer measures (those with the lowest degree of association) can be eliminated in subsequent research.

Implementation of these steps should result in greater comparability of research findings. This, in turn, will enhance our ability to assess the state of knowledge at any given time and should ultimately lead to an increased ability to predict academic performance.

The Independence of Predictor Measures

We turn now from the question of measures with similar labels that may actually be measuring different content to its obverse, the question of the degree of independence of measures purporting to measure different phenomena.

As succeeding chapters will indicate, a rather large number of variables appear to be useful in the prediction of academic performance. However, while they have different conceptual labels, closer examination reveals that they may not always be independent of one another. For example, many studies use interest inventories as predictors of academic performance. The basic idea is that if a student is equally talented in two subject areas, his level of performance should be higher in the subject for which his interest is greater. However, there is some evidence that over-achieving students tend to have higher interest scores in areas related to high prestige occupations. If this is the case, we may raise the question as to whether interests may not be an indirect way of measuring social mobility aspirations (the desire to "get ahead" in the world). To put it another way, interest measures may not be independent of measures of social aspiration level.

To the extent that there are variables with different labels which are not independent of one another, it might be erroneously concluded that there are a larger number of predictor variables that seem promising than in fact there are. One may assert that to argue about what these variables should be called is merely playing with words. However, a large number of concepts are used in these prediction studies, and the boundaries of meaning are not well delineated. One index of usefulness of a variable in such research is that it make an independent contribution to the prediction of performance. If a variable does not meet this standard, it should be either eliminated or classed with other predictor variables with which it is correlated. There are many variables presently in use that seem to have some underlying similarities even though they are differently labeled.

This state of affairs has arisen primarily because most studies use only one or two variables for the prediction of academic performance. We need more studies that use a larger number of variables. These would allow us to evaluate the independence of each variable, and in the long run they would probably result in the use of a smaller number of predictors, since many variables that were not independent of one another would be classified together.

INTERPRETATION OF RELATIONSHIPS BETWEEN PREDICTORS AND PERFORMANCE CRITERIA

This section concerns three problems regarding the interpretation of relationships between predictors and academic performance. The first involves types of association between the two; the second, some problems of interpretation when relationships are of either very high or very low magnitude; and finally, the question of the causal status of predictor variables.

The Assumption of Linearity in Prediction

In many studies concerning the prediction of academic performance, the relationship between a predictor variable and the criterion is assessed by means of correlational analysis. In almost all of these studies, the correlation methods assume linear relationships—that is, they assume that unit increases in the predictor variable will be followed by unit increases (or decreases in the case of negative relationships) in the criterion, and that this will occur along the entire distribution of scores. For example, if intelligence is used to predict academic performance, the usual correlation methods assume that the overall correlation is equally representative at all levels of intelligence. That is, the correlation would hold for IQ's of 130 and above just as well as it would hold for IQ's of 110 and below. However, when one considers the degree of relationship between ability and performance at different segments of the ability range, he may find that ability measures are predictive at some segments of the range but not at others, and/or that they are predictive only up to a certain point. As McClelland has put it:

> Let us admit that morons cannot do good school work. But what evidence is there that intelligence is not a threshold type of variable, that once a person has a certain minimal level of intelligence his performance beyond that point is uncorrelated with his ability? Several studies suggest that if such a minimal level is set fairly high, ability may no longer play a crucial role in success. Ann Roe in her study of eminent scientists has reported intelligence test data showing a wide range from the highest to the lowest person tested. It is true that the *average* score was very high, but it is equally true that there were several scientists whose tested intelligence was only moderately above average. In other words, given a certain moderately high level of intelligence, it is possible to be one of the world's greatest living scientists.[1]

Thus, as McClelland goes on to suggest, ability and performance measures should be plotted carefully so that increase, decrease, or threshold characteristics of intelligence in relation to performance at different segments of the intelligence range can be observed. To the extent that diminished relations or threshold phenomena are found, the investigator must then turn his attention to other nonintellective factors that might account for variations in academic performance. The significance of this point extends beyond ability tests as predictors. It applies to any variable that is used for prediction purposes.

In addition to the question of threshold effects, the exclusive use of linear correlation methods hinders the discovery of curvilinear relationships between predictors and academic performance. In illustration, consider a personality variable such as test-taking anxiety. It might be that very low levels of anxiety result in low levels of performance on examinations, moderate levels of anxiety lead to high levels of performance, and very high levels of anxiety lead to poor test performance. If this were found to be the case, a linear correlation coefficient could not accurately reflect the true state of affairs. Future research should be addressed to the problem of discovering those instances in which the relation of a personality variable to academic achievement is characteristically curvilinear rather than linear.

Interpreting Relationships of Extreme Magnitude

Correlations between predictors and academic performance are frequently low and only occasionally very high. Either case presents a problem of the inferences to be drawn. If the relationship is high, say of the order of .80 or above, one may ask why it is necessary to research further—why go on to investigate additional variables when in all likelihood one may have attained the upper limit of predictability, and all that remains lies in the domain of measurement error? If the relationship is very low, a question arises as to whether the predictor should continue to be used, since its efficiency is open to question.

There are at least three answers to these questions. First, whether associations are very low or very high, it is always necessary to replicate, since the stability of findings cannot be assessed from just one study. Thus, if a very high correlation is observed, replication allows the assessment of the consistency of the finding. In like manner, if a low correlation is found, one should not abandon the predictor variable until replication clearly establishes the stability of the finding. Even in the latter case, it is questionable whether such a predictor should be discarded, for the observation of even a small relationship is useful to a degree.

Second, even with correlations as high as .80, more than a third of the variation in performance criteria remains unexplained. While much of this unexplained variation may be attributable to measurement error in the predictor and/or the criterion, as we have indicated earlier, a portion of this error (such as variations in course distributions, variations in teachers' grading habits, and the like) may be theoretically meaningful.

Third, high statistical associations do not automatically shed light on the theoretical interpretations explaining the relationships. High correlations do not necessarily indicate that the predictors are causally related to the criterion. This point is especially relevant to research on academic achievement, because many predictors are ambiguous in their causal status. Let us take a closer look at this issue.

Interpreting the Causal Status of Predictor Variables

When a significant association is found between some predictive variable and academic performance, the question arises as to whether the predictor is a determinant of performance in the causal sense.

For example, suppose that a researcher is interested in assessing the relationship between sociometric status, as indexed by popularity with classmates, and academic performance, and that the data show a positive correlation between the two. That is, the more popular a student is with his classmates, the higher will be his academic performance. There are at least three possible interpretations of this finding. First, popularity might, in fact, be a determinant of performance. The argument here might be that being unpopular arouses anxiety and that this, in turn, interferes with good school work. A second interpretation might be that popularity is a result rather than a determinant of performance.

Under this interpretation, we could say that those whose school performance is of high quality are looked up to by their peers, perhaps because there is a peer group norm that rewards high performance. A third interpretation could be that both academic performance and popularity are jointly determined by some third, unknown factor that was not measured in the study. In short, the observation of an association between two variables does not, in itself, establish the presence of a causal relationship.

In field investigations, such as research on academic achievement, it is, of course, always difficult to establish causal interpretations because it is not possible to control extraneous factors with the precision often attainable in the laboratory setting. However, certain steps can be taken that at least help to support the validity of causal interpretations. One procedure involves the establishment of time sequences among variables. It follows from the assumption that in a causal relationship, the independent or causal factor will precede the dependent factor in time. Thus, if popularity can be shown to precede scholastic standing, this would lend support to the interpretation that popularity is a determinant of the latter. On the other hand, if it can be shown that the sociometric structure of a classroom group does not crystallize until *after* the scholastic standing of the students is known, then popularity could not be viewed as a causal factor.

While determination of proper time sequence helps to support causal interpretations, it does not establish them with certainty. There are at least two reasons for this. First, even if the predictor variable is shown to precede the criterion, the correlation may still be determined by another unknown factor. Second, even if a personality variable is a useful predictor of academic performance in college, the characteristic itself may have been determined, in part, by academic performance at preceding educational levels. For example, if high self-confidence is associated with high academic achievement in college, it is possible that confidence is a result of earlier successful performance in high school.

The example above points up something that is usually overlooked in research; namely, that many relationships are not of the simple, mechanistic, cause-and-effect variety. Instead, some variables may have a mutual effect upon one another. That is, an increase in one variable may result in an increase in the second variable, and the second variable, in turn, may bring about a further increase in the first variable. In short, we would have an interdependent or feedback relationship.[2] To illustrate using the earlier example, high self-confidence may lead to high performance, which, in turn, leads to higher confidence, and this leads to an even higher level of performance. Processes of this kind are of more than rhetorical interest, because they may be closely related to academic failure for many students. Thus, poor performance may sometimes lead to lower confidence, which may reduce future performance, and so on, until a vicious circle is formed, with the result that the student becomes demoralized and fails to achieve at even minimal levels.

The preceding discussion tries to indicate that those studies that implicitly assume causal status for predictors are on tenuous ground. However, many studies simply are not concerned with the question of causality. Rather, they aim to discover correlates of academic performance and to use these for prediction purposes. There is ample evidence that the discovery of predictive factors may be useful on practical grounds, even if these factors have no causal significance. For example, automobile insurance rates are determined partly on the basis of a negative relation between age and accident rates—that is, the lower the age of drivers, the higher the accident rate. Such data are certainly useful, yet it would be absurd to argue that age, in itself, causes accidents. In educational research many predictive variables are of this type. Thus, academic performance in high school is consistently one of the best predictors of performance in college; yet no one would argue that high school grades are a cause of college performance. That high school grades are highly related to college grades tells us only that whatever variables account for performance in high school probably are operative also on the college level. While it is both important and interesting to know that high school and college situations may be more alike than some may think, this finding does not increase our understanding of what accounts for performance differences in either situation.

The findings only further stimulate our curiosity about the types of factors that might be involved in performance at both educational levels.

The type of search for predictor variables that is little concerned with why they are predictive might be called the "actuarial" approach. On this level the discovery of predictive factors comes mainly from common sense or from intuition. It now seems likely that we may have reached the limits of predictive efficiency attainable through the actuarial approach. Further progress may come only through more systematic theorizing about the determinants of academic performance. This will involve thinking about why certain variables are predictive, rather than being content with only the demonstration that they do predict.

CHARACTERISTICS OF STUDY DESIGNS

We turn now to a consideration of two problems involving the characteristics of research designs.[3] The first concerns the question of the control or lack of control of certain important study variables. The second pertains to the question of static versus longitudinal designs in the study of academic performance.

Control Variables in the Study of Academic Performance

As we shall see in the chapters that follow, three factors emerge as basic correlates of academic performance. These are ability, sex, and socioeconomic status (hereafter referred to as SES). We call these "basic" correlates not because they are theoretically more significant than other variables, but because they are related to performance more consistently. Thus, ability is directly related to school performance; females have higher levels of academic achievement than males; and students of higher SES perform at higher levels than students of lower SES. Failure to control for these factors in studies of academic performance may lead to a number of difficulties. The problems of controlling for ability already have been discussed in Chapter 2. We now consider the two other factors, sex and SES.

There are two reasons for controlling for the sex of the student in studies of academic performance. In the first place, evidence to be presented in Chapter 4 suggests that ability and school performance are more highly correlated for females than for males. In addition, the absolute level of performance tends to be higher for females. This means that when males and females are not separated in analysis, the magnitude of correlations between ability and school performance will not accurately reflect the true level for the sexes separately.

In the second place, the variables that predict performance for males may be different from the variables that are predictive for females, and even if the same variables are involved for both sexes, the direction of the relationships might differ (it might be positive for males and negative for females). If the sexes are not separated, these possibilities are obscured. Moreover, the failure to control for sex differences contributes to our present ignorance concerning the sources of these differences in academic performance. For these reasons, it is important to perform separate analyses for each sex.

Socioeconomic status consistently exhibits a positive association with academic performance. What is the theoretical significance of this finding? The most likely interpretation is that SES is a variable that summarizes a variety of personality characteristics. That is, evidence (to be presented in Chapter 6) suggests that the social classes differ in terms of behavioral patterns such as child-rearing practices. These patterns, in turn, may be determinants of personality characteristics and values that are related to academic achievement. Thus, the observation of differences in academic performance according to SES should sensitize us to the kinds of personality variables that are relevant.

Static Versus Longitudinal Designs

With few exceptions, studies of academic performance are of static rather than longitudinal design. The static design deals with the prediction of performance at one point in time. Illustrative would be research concerned with the prediction of grades for the first semester of the freshman year of college. Longitudinal studies, on the other hand, deal with performance at several points in time.

Because research is overwhelmingly of the static type, we know very little about the answers to a number of interesting questions that can be explored only through longitudinal studies. Thus, such research can shed light on the degree of variability of academic performance through time. For example, longitudinal research can assess the consistency of academic performance from the freshman through senior years of college as well as through different educational levels. This type of study can find variables that may be useful predictors at one time or educational level but do not predict at a later time or different educational level. Thus, longitudinal studies also allow us to deal with the question of the stability of predictor variables through time. To the extent that change is observed in predictors and/or performance, new theoretical questions are raised concerning the determinants of such changes.

Longitudinal studies are valuable also because they allow us to investigate interdependent or feedback relationships. Only through the measurement of performance and predictors at several points in time can such relationships be discovered.

Besides being theoretically interesting in themselves, answers to these kinds of questions have practical significance. College admissions officers and guidance personnel are certainly interested in predicting more than a student's grades during freshman year. It would be valuable to be able to predict the level of performance throughout the college career because a student's performance may fluctuate widely in quality. If this type of performance were predictable, and if it were possible to know whether or not future performance was likely to improve, educational administrators would be in a position to make sounder decisions. More longitudinal research may provide some answers for these problems.

SUMMARY

This chapter has introduced a number of questions important to a review and critical appraisal of research on academic achievement. One set of difficulties involves the predictors of academic performance, including the poor standardization of predictors and the fact that different predictors are often not independent of one another.

An important problem regarding the interpretation of relationships between predictors and criteria of academic performance involves the question of causality. A significant relationship between predictor and criterion does not necessarily establish that the predictor is a causal determinant of the criterion. In addition, there is a tendency to assume that relationships are linear and to ignore the possibility that they are curvilinear or interdependent.

Certain characteristics of study designs have been considered. One issue involved the implications of failure to control for basic correlates of academic performance such as ability, sex, and socioeconomic status. A second issue involved the preponderance of studies with a static rather than longitudinal design. Longitudinal designs are able to deal with a number of significant questions that cannot be investigated in static designs.

The presentation of these issues provides a context for the assessment of research on academic performance. We now turn to this literature.

NOTES TO CHAPTER 3

1. McClelland, David C., "Issues in the Identification of Talent" in McClelland, David C., and associates, *Talent and Society,* D. Van Nostrand Co., Inc., Princeton, N.J., 1958, pp. 12–13. The allusion to Ann Roe refers to the following: Roe, Ann, *The Making of a Scientist,* Dodd, Mead and Co., New York, 1953.

2. A discussion of this type of relationship is presented in Zetterberg, Hans L., *On Theory and Verification in Sociology,* rev. ed., The Bedminster Press, Totowa, N.J., 1963, chap. 2.

3. This section is not intended as a complete, detailed analysis of design considerations in educational research. For an excellent detailed presentation, see the chapter entitled "Experimental and Quasi-Experimental Designs for Research on Teaching," by Donald T. Campbell and Julian C. Stanley, in Gage, N. L., editor, *Handbook of Research on Teaching,* Rand McNally and Co., Chicago, 1963, chap. 5.

Chapter 4

Intellective Factors as Predictors

THIS CHAPTER deals with measures of intellectual ability as predictors of academic performance. It begins with a brief discussion of the meaning of intelligence, continues with a classification of the various types of studies and a review of the findings, and ends with a summary and an evaluation of the current status of this work.

THE MEANING OF INTELLIGENCE

Before turning to the literature on the relationship between intellectual ability and academic performance, we wish first to discuss the meaning of intelligence. The issues surrounding this question are quite complex and have been subject to controversy for a long time. It would require a very extended treatment to explore them adequately. For this reason we shall merely summarize a few of the main points.

Most persons would agree that intelligence and ability tests measure dimensions of problem-solving capacity. However, there is much less agreement regarding the *sources* of this capacity. Theoretical positions on this topic can be summarized under three headings: first is the position that the intelligence test score is an index of inherited ability; second is the environmentalist view that intelligence is largely a product of cultural factors; and finally, there is the opinion that intelligence level is determined by the interaction of hereditary and environmental factors. The last position now has the support of most social scientists, although this orientation includes two factions, one maintaining that environment is relatively more important and the other that heredity is more significant.[1]

While this question is not fully resolved at present, it is clear that inherited ability is only one factor determining an intelligence test score. The various factors that may be influential have been described in a recent volume by Goslin:

> A person's test score reflects a number of different factors. . . . The major . . . variables [are] . . . the individual's inherited potential, both in terms of (1) general intelligence and (2) specific capacities for training . . . , plus the environment in which the organism has developed. Within the general category of environmental influences, [are] . . . the effects of (3) the individual's cultural background . . . , (4) his formal training experiences (school, and the like), (5) his experiences with similar tests, and (6) his general health. . . .
>
> Intervening between the test score and [these] variables [are] . . . four major sources of fluctuation in performance: personality, situation, test demands, and random variation. The major personality variables [are] . . . (7) achievement motivation, (8) interest of the individual in the . . . test, and (9) anxiety connected with the testing situation. The situational factors [are] . . . (10) the perceived importance of the test, (11) the confidence of the individual in his ability to handle the test items, (12) the specific physical condition of the examinee at the time of the test administration, (13) interference from the environment during test administration, and (14) the effect of the tester. Evaluated under the general heading of test demands [are] (15) the influence of the specific kinds of learning or abilities required by the test, (16) the demands of the test with respect to the speed of response required of the examinee, and (17) the role played by misleading or faultily constructed items. Finally, the random variation produced by (18) guessing and (19) clerical errors [are] considered.[2]

Whatever may be the relative importance of these factors in determining ability scores, success in school requires, in part, certain cognitive skills. Moreover, these skills are measured, to a significant degree, by intelligence tests. For this reason, these tests are moderately successful in predicting academic performance.

CLASSIFICATION OF STUDIES

Studies that use ability measures to predict academic performance exhibit considerable variation. To assure that findings will be comparable, we will note these variations and organize the literature in terms of them.

A major respect in which studies vary is in their concern with global as against multidimensional prediction. This distinction is applicable to the criteria of academic performance as well as to the predictors. By global predictors or criteria, we refer to the use of a single, overall measure of ability and/or academic performance. Illustrative would be the total score on an intelligence test and the overall grade-point average. Multidimensional predictors or criteria refer to the use of a number of specific dimensions of ability and/or performance. Illustrative would be the subscores of a profile abilities test and the computation of grades for separate courses or course areas.

These distinctions are illustrated in Chart 2, which shows that there are four general types of studies. Cell A portrays the type of study where a single index of ability is used to predict a single, overall index of academic performance. In cell B, a global measure of ability is used to predict performance in separate courses or course areas. This type of study does not occur frequently. Cell C depicts studies that use a number of dimensions of ability to predict a global measure of performance. Cell D represents the situation where different ability dimensions are used for the prediction of performance in specific courses or course areas. Actually, two kinds of studies can be classified

CHART 2. TYPES OF STUDIES RELATING ABILITY AND ACADEMIC PERFORMANCE

Predictor	Criterion	
	Global	Multidimensional
Global	Global ability measure used to predict grade-point average (A)	Global ability measure used to predict grades in specific courses (B)
Multi-dimensional	Several specific ability dimensions used to predict grade-point average (C)	Several specific ability dimensions used to predict grades in specific courses (D)

within cell D: first, a uniform battery of predictor variables may be used for predicting grades in different courses; second, the composition of the predictor battery may be changed according to the particular course for which grades are being predicted. In the latter case, the basis for change is predictive efficiency. That is, the particular combination of intellective variables used is the one that yields the highest correlation with a given course grade. This method is known as the differential prediction technique.

Studies also vary according to educational level. Here we distinguish between studies of performance in the elementary, high school, college, and graduate school settings.

Another kind of variation in the research involves the sex composition of study samples. Some studies use all male samples; some use all females; others are mixed. Within the last group, some control this factor by reporting findings separately for each sex, and others do not.

The findings will be reported separately for each of these variations.

THE RESEARCH FINDINGS

The Graduate School Level

Only a few published studies of the academic performance of graduate students have been found. One global investigation (cell A of Chart 2) used scores on the Miller Analogies Test as a predictor of grade-point average for graduate students in education.[3] This measure correlated .21 with grades.

Of two multiple prediction studies (cell C), one used the Miller Analogies Test, the undergraduate average, and a mathematical reasoning test for the prediction of grades in a graduate statistics department.[4] The multiple correlation of these measures with graduate grades was .43. For a group of graduate students in psychology, grade-point averages were predicted at about .60, using a combination of scores on a comprehensive examination in 10 areas of psychology, plus undergraduate science grades.[5] In this study, the Miller Analogies Test was not a good predictor.

Webb used three measures (undergraduate grades, Cooperative General Culture Test, and Cooperative English Test) for the prediction of success in graduate school.[6] He defined success in terms of a number of criteria such as graduate average and ratings on research ability. The zero-order correlations ranged from about .20 to .35. No multiple correlations were reported.

These studies indicate that the predictability of performance for graduate school is generally lower than for the college level. This is probably because graduate students are a more highly selected group than undergraduates—the range of intellectual ability in graduate school is usually considerably narrower as well as of higher quality. Since there is less variation in ability, the correlations are smaller. Moreover, some of the tests used as predictors are often used as screening devices in graduate admissions. In particular, the Miller Analogies Test is sometimes used in this way. Because of this, it is not surprising that this measure has only low correlations with performance.

The College Level

We deal first with global measures of ability and performance represented in cell A. The literature here is voluminous. The presentation to follow is limited to summaries of the studies made prior to 1953 and to a review of those reported through 1961.

Cronbach in an earlier review (1949) reports that on the college level ability tests correlate about .50 to .55 with grade-point averages.[7] A review by Henry in 1950 arrives at a similar conclusion.[8] More recent research also indicates that the correlations average about .50,[9] with a range of about .30 to .70. Part of this variation is probably due to the use of different types of ability measures. Some studies use one of the standard intelligence tests, and others use tests intended specifically as predictors of school performance such as the Scholastic Aptitude Test developed by Educational Testing Service. A third index of ability involves measures of prior scholastic performance as predictors of future performance. A common example is the use of high school grades to predict college grades. While it has been conventional to use the high school grade as an ability measure for predicting college performance, it should be noted that ability is not the only factor determining the high school record. Numerous personality and social factors are involved.

Another reason for discrepancies in results, in addition to the use of different ability tests, is the differing sex composition of study samples. In some studies correlations are computed for both sexes combined; in others the sample consists entirely of males or females. Where correlations are computed separately, a sex difference is suggested.[10] With only one exception[11] these latter studies show that correlations are higher for females than for males.

We turn now to studies of the type portrayed in cell C of Chart 2—that is, studies in which a battery of predictors is used to predict an overall index of college performance. Cronbach reported in 1949 that multiple correlations of such batteries with college grade-point average run at about .60 to .70.[12] Recent research is in line with this conclusion, showing an average correlation of about .65.[13] Thus, the magnitude of prediction is higher in this type of study than in the global type.

Of all the measures used in these prediction batteries, the one that consistently emerges as the best single predictor is the high school average or high school rank. Illustrative is a study by Swensen.[14] He found that students in the upper two-fifths of their graduating class in high school received significantly higher grades at the end of the first semester of college than students who graduated in the lower three-fifths of their high school class, even though these two groups did not differ on a standard aptitude test.

Only a few studies using batteries of predictors present data on sex differences.[15] Two show that multiple correlations for females are higher than for males, and two show no sex difference. None of these investigations indicates that males are higher than females. This again suggests that females tend to be more predictable than males in academic performance.

We now present the findings from studies corresponding to cell D of Chart 2, where the approach is to use several dimensions of aptitude for the prediction of grades in specific courses or course areas. When the content of predictor batteries varies depending on the particular course for which grades are being predicted, this is referred to as the differential prediction technique.

Horst has contributed greatly to the development of this technique.[16] His work is based on the rationale that while global predictors and criteria emphasize overall academic performance, it is probable that the performance of most students differs qualitatively from one subject area to another. That is, most students are good in some things and not so good in others. Furthermore, because of the specialized nature of our occupational system, people must choose to do one thing rather than many things. Thus, it is of practical importance to isolate those abilities on which they are high and those subjects in which they do well. Whereas global prediction cannot tackle this problem, differential prediction can deal with it.

Horst has used this technique on a number of samples at the University of Washington. Median correlations are generally at about the .50 level, with some correlations as low as .13 and others as high as .89.[17] Other studies support the usefulness of the approach. Travers suggests that measures of verbal abilities correlate more highly with grades for English and foreign language than with grades for mathematics, and that quantitative ability correlates more highly with grades for mathematics subjects.[18] An investigation by Fisher showed that for the differential prediction of grades in mathematics, science, and social studies, the most effective predictive variables were the parallel content areas of the predictive tests.[19] Anderson found that unique predictive batteries existed for students in different curriculum groups.[20]

A number of findings contradict these, however. Cronbach asserts that multifactor tests of abilities add little to the prediction of performance in particular courses beyond what the general intelligence factor will predict.[21] Berdie found only limited success in predicting grades in various kinds of courses from differential abilities measures.[22] Eells found that differential batteries yielded higher multiple correlations with grades in different curricula than did a single, uniform test battery.[23] However, he concludes that the use of a differential battery rather than a uniform battery is not justified, since the difference between the two was not large enough to warrant the additional effort involved in using the former.

The findings regarding differential prediction are inconsistent. One reason for their apparent contradictions may be differences in the definitions of criteria. Thus, some researchers try to predict differentially for curricular groupings. That is, they try to discover the batteries most efficient for the prediction of overall performance in different curricula, such as liberal arts, engineering, and so on. Others attempt to predict grades in specific courses. In addition, the content of the predictive batteries varies from one study to another. Furthermore, most of the studies do not make explicit comparisons of the relative effectiveness of differential versus uniform batteries, or of batteries versus global predictive instruments. Thus, even though a particular differential prediction study may obtain fairly high correlations, we do not know whether these correlations are significantly higher than those which could be obtained using global predictors or uniform test batteries. Considerably more research needs to be done before these matters can be clarified.

Turning to the question of sex differences, only one of these differential prediction studies reports its findings separately for males and females. In this study, the correlations for females are higher than for males.[24]

In addition to the preceding research there are two other studies that cannot be classified in terms of Chart 2. They are cited because of their novel approach.

One study by Berdie was concerned with the assessment of intra-individual variability as a predictor of grades.[25] The procedure was to obtain 10 subscores of a mathematics test and to classify students at a technology school into high- and low-variability groups. He categorized those students who exhibited considerable variation from one subscore to another as the high group and students whose 10 subscores were quite consistent as the low group. He hypothesized that the high variability group would be less predictable on grades than the low group. The findings indicated that among high-ability students, those who showed high variability were less predictable than those who showed low variability. Among students of lower ability, variability was unrelated to grades.

In another study, Forehand and McQuitty attempted to assess whether prediction could be improved by using a "configuration" of predictors.[26] In configuration analysis, *patterns* of responses are used as predictors. Eleven aptitude, achievement, and interest scales were factor analyzed, and the patterns of standings on the factors were used to predict grades. What is meant by "patterns" of standings on factors can be illustrated by the following example: Suppose that there were three factors and that one student scored high on the first and second but low on the third, another scored low on the first two but high on the third. In this case each student exhibited a distinct pattern or configuration. The findings showed that this method resulted in higher correlations with academic performance than the usual multiple correlation analysis. However, on a second study sample, correlations from the configural analysis were considerably smaller than for the first sample; while the multiple correlation analysis did not exhibit this shrinkage.

The theoretical significance of these two last-mentioned studies is not clear, but their novel approach and suggestive findings indicate that they deserve further investigation.

The High School Level

First we review global measures of ability and performance, as in cell A of Chart 2. Cronbach reported one study in which correlations between intelligence and grades were .55.[27] Travers found that correlations between intelligence and grades ran between .50 and .75 on the eighth- to tenth-grade levels.[28] Gough obtained correlations of from .62 to .80 with three samples of high school seniors, and Friedhoff obtained a correlation of .44 with an eighth-grade sample.[29] Carter found correlations of about .60 for three samples, and Jacobs obtained similar findings.[30] In a study of gifted high school students, Nason observed correlations of .34 for boys and .39 for girls, using intelligence as a predictor of grades.[31] These last correlations are lower than for the other samples, probably because of the narrow intelligence distribution of the sample.

These studies suggest that for the high school level, ability and grades are correlated at about .60. This is somewhat higher than the findings for the college level where the average correlation is about .50. In all probability this difference is due primarily to the wider range of ability on the high school level. On the college level, admissions procedures tend to eliminate those of low ability. As the ability range becomes narrower, correlations with performance are likely to decrease.

In the two studies mentioned above that explicitly compared males and females,[32] correlations for females were higher than for males.

In a study that used a battery of predictors (cell C), Wellman found a multiple correlation of about .80.[33]

Three studies utilize differential prediction. Mitchell found that a four-factor ability test predicted differentially for achievement tests in specific content areas as well as for grades in specific courses.[34] In general, the predictions were better when achievement tests were used as criteria of performance than when grades were used. Another investigation found that multidimensional tests of abilities do not necessarily predict most highly for the content areas in which they would be expected to predict.[35] In this study the highest correlations were of the order of .50. This is lower than obtained with the use of global predictors. A third study found that differential aptitude measures are not superior to global ability measures for the prediction of grades in specific courses.[36]

The status of differential prediction on the high school level is similar to that on the college level. That is, the evidence does not indicate that differential prediction is superior to the other methods reviewed here. With regard to sex differences, correlations tend to be higher for females than for males in the differential prediction studies which control on this factor.

The Elementary School Level

Research on this level is less frequent than for any other. In one study intelligence was correlated with grades in various subject areas, using a group of students for whom data were available for grades 2 through 7.[37] Grades consisted of qualitative evaluations (good, fair, and so on). Correlations were found to be quite consistent from grades 2 through 7, averaging around .65. In another study, Barnes correlated intelligence scores with scores on subtests of an achievement measure for students in grades 1 through 4.[38] The correlations ranged from .31 to .63 and showed a tendency to increase from first to second grade. However, the magnitude of the correlations seemed fairly stable from the second through the fourth grade. In neither study are the data analyzed separately for each sex.

The findings from the Barnes study regarding the increase in correlations from first to second grade suggest the possibility of an age effect or perhaps a more complex process of "crystallization" of performance after the first grade. The question of the stability of performance at the outset of the educational career seems especially interesting and deserving of more research.

SUMMARY AND EVALUATION

The preceding research findings may be summarized in terms of three factors: the type of analysis (as in Chart 2), the educational level, and the sex differences.

The research shows that the best predictions are obtained from multiple correlations in which a battery of intellective variables is used to predict the overall grade-point average (cell C of Chart 2). Studies using a global ability measure to predict overall school performance (cell A) obtain somewhat lower correlations. In both types of studies the single best predictor of performance on the college level is the high school academic record. However, this is due in part to the fact that high school grades are determined by many factors in addition to measured intellectual ability. The results of studies using the differential prediction approach are not consistent primarily because much of the research is not comparable.

Of all educational levels, the highest correlations are obtained for the high school level; the college level ranks next; and the graduate level is lowest. Data for elementary school students are too scarce to allow a meaningful generalization. The greater association between ability and performance in high school as compared with other levels is probably the result of the wider ability distribution at that level.

While many studies do not present data separately for males and females, those that do find that correlations between ability and performance are higher for females.[39] This finding holds mainly for the high school and college levels. At other levels the data are too few to allow an assessment of sex differences.

Some of the issues described in Chapter 3 are pertinent to the studies reviewed here. In the first place, insufficient research has been done on the graduate and elementary levels. Because of this, findings on these levels are less definitive.

Second, the failure of many studies to analyze data separately for males and females hinders comparability among investigations. More research is needed in which sex differences are assessed and in which the reasons for these differences are examined.

Third, more longitudinal studies are needed. Almost all studies predict academic performance at only one point in time. For example, most research on college performance is actually concerned with the prediction of grades in the freshman year. As a result, we are ignorant regarding the consistency of performance and the degree to which it is predictable over time.

A fourth problem concerns the question of linearity in prediction. From Chapter 3 we recall that ability may be a threshold variable. That is, after a certain level is reached, ability may no longer play a significant role in predicting school performance, so that performance may then have to be accounted for through the use of nonintellective factors. Thus, the relatively low predictive usefulness of ability factors in graduate school is perhaps accounted for by the fact that ability levels here are generally quite high, so poor performance cannot be explained as a function of ability. Research is needed in which the relationships between performance and different segments of the range of ability are examined. In this way threshold effects can be assessed, and our knowledge of the relations between ability and academic performance will become more precise.

In spite of the presence of these unfinished tasks, it is true that on those educational levels for which data are most reliable (high school and college) measures of ability on the average account for 35 to 45 per cent of the variation in academic performance. While no other single type of factor accounts for this much variation, more than half still remains unexplained. Thus, attention turns to other factors of a nonintellective nature which may be pertinent. The three remaining chapters focus upon these.

NOTES TO CHAPTER 4

1. For a presentation of the environmental position, see the study by Kenneth Eells and associates, *Intelligence and Cultural Differences,* University of Chicago Press, Chicago, 1951. The genetic view is presented by Cyril Burt, "The Inheritance of Mental Ability," *The American Psychologist,* vol. 13, 1958, pp. 1–15. A detailed consideration of the question is provided by Joseph McVicker Hunt, *Intelligence and Experience,* The Ronald Press Co., New York, 1961.

2. Goslin, David A., *The Search for Ability: Standardized Testing in Social Perspective.* Russell Sage Foundation, New York, 1963, pp. 151–152.

3. Durnall, Edward J., Jr., "Predicting Scholastic Success for Graduate Students in Education," *School and Society,* vol. 80, 1954, p. 107.

4. Schwartz, Milton M., and F. Eugene Clark, "Prediction of Success in Graduate School at Rutgers University," *Journal of Educational Research,* vol. 53, 1959, pp. 109–111.

5. Platz, Arthur, Charles McClintock, and Daniel Katz, "Undergraduate Grades and the Miller Analogies Test as Predictors of Graduate Success," *American Psychologist,* vol. 14, 1959, pp. 285–289.

6. Webb, Sam C., "Differential Prediction of Success in a Graduate School," *Journal of Educational Research,* vol. 50, 1956, pp. 45–54.

7. Cronbach, Lee J., *Essentials of Psychological Testing,* Harper and Brothers, New York, 1949.

8. Henry, Erwin R., "Predicting Success in College and University" in Fryer, Douglas H., and Erwin R. Henry, editors, *Handbook of Applied Psychology.* Rinehart and Co., New York, 1950, pp. 449–453.

9. Anderson, Mary R., and Erwin J. Stegman, "Predictors of Freshman Achievement at Fort Hays Kansas State College," *Educational and Psychological Measurement,* vol. 14, 1954, pp. 722–723; Bergeron, Wilbur L., "An Analysis of the Relationship Between Selected Characteristics and Academic Success of Freshmen at the University of Arkansas," *Dissertation Abstracts,* vol. 13, 1953, p. 505; Boyd, Joseph D., "The Relative Prognostic Value of Selected Criteria in Predicting Academic Success at Northwestern University," *Dissertation Abstracts,* vol. 15, 1955, p. 1780; Brice, Marshall M., "A Comparison of Subjective Predictions with Objective Predictions of College Achievement," *Dissertation Abstracts,* vol. 16, 1956, p. 1622; Frick, J. W., "Improving the Prediction of Academic Achievement by Use of the MMPI," *Journal of Applied Psychology,* vol. 39, 1955, pp. 49–52; Frick, J. W., and Helen E. Kenner, "A Validation Study of the Prediction of College Achievement," *Journal of Applied Psychology,* vol. 40, 1956, pp. 251–252; Henderson, Harold L., "Prediction of Academic Success," *Psychological Reports,* vol. 2, 1956, pp. 321–322; Klugh, Henry E., and Robert Bierley, "The School and College Ability Test and High School Grades as Predictors of College Achievement," *Educational and Psychological Measurement,* vol. 19, 1959, pp. 625–626; Klugh, Henry E., and Albert W. Bendig, "The Manifest Anxiety and ACE Scales and College Achievement," *Journal of Consulting Psychology,* vol. 19, 1955, p. 487; O'Neill, Ralph C., "Predicting College Success with the ITED (Iowa Tests of Educational Development)," *California Journal of Educational Research,* vol. 10, 1959, pp. 86–89; Scannell, Dale P., "Prediction of College Success from Elementary and Secondary School Performance," *Journal of Educational Psychology,* vol. 51, 1960, pp. 130–135; Schutter, Genevieve, and Howard Maher, "Predicting Grade-Point Average with a Forced-Choice Study Activity Questionnaire," *Journal of Applied Psychology,* vol. 40, 1956, pp. 253–257; Sharp, Heber Cannon, and L. M. Pickett, "The General Aptitude Test Battery as a Predictor of College Success," *Educational and Psychological Measurement,* vol. 19, 1959, pp. 617–623.

10. Abelson, Robert P., "Sex Differences in Predictability of College Grades," *Educational and Psychological Measurement,* vol. 12, 1952, pp. 638–644; Boyd, Joseph D., *op. cit.;* Jackson, Robert A., "Prediction of the Academic Success of College Freshmen," *Journal of Educational Psychology,* vol. 46, 1955, pp. 296–301; Klugh, Henry E. and Robert Bierley, *op. cit.;* Scannell, Dale P., *op. cit.*

11. Boyd, Joseph D., *op. cit.*

12. Cronbach, Lee J., *op. cit.*

13. Anderson, Mary R., and Erwin J. Stegman, *op. cit.;* Bonner, Leon, "Factors Associated with the Academic Achievement of Freshmen Students at a Southern Agricultural College," *Dissertation Abstracts,* vol. 17, 1957, pp. 266–267; Boyer, Roscoe A., "A Study of the Academic Success of Undergraduate Students as Identified by Aptitude Test Profiles," *Dissertation Abstracts,* vol. 17, 1957, pp. 89–90; Boyd, Joseph D., *op. cit.;* Brice, Marshall M., *op. cit.;* Bruce, William J., "The Contribution of

Eleven Variables to the Prognosis of Academic Success at the University of Washington," *Dissertation Abstracts,* vol. 13, 1953, pp. 505–506; Chahbazi, Parviz, "Analysis of Cornell Orientation Inventory Items on Study Habits and Their Relative Value in Prediction of College Achievement," *Journal of Experimental Education,* vol. 27, 1958, pp. 135–142; Chapman, Harold M., "The Prediction of Freshman Scholarship from a Combination of Standardized Test Scores and High School Grades," *Dissertation Abstracts,* vol. 15, 1955, p. 1201; Chappell, Tolan L., "Differential Prediction of Achievement at the University of Missouri," *Educational and Psychological Measurement,* vol. 14, 1954, pp. 724–725; Fisher, Joseph T., "The Value of Tests and Records in the Prediction of College Achievement," *Dissertation Abstracts,* vol. 15, 1955, p. 2097; Fishman, Joshua A., *Research Activities of the College Entrance Examination Board, 1952–1957,* College Entrance Examination Board, New York, 1958 (mimeo.); Fitzgibbon, Thomas J., "The Prediction of Academic Success of Freshmen at Bradley University," *Dissertation Abstracts,* vol. 14, 1954, p. 1170; Franz, Gretchen, Junius Davis, and Dolores Garcia, "Prediction of Grades from Preadmissions Indices in Georgia Taxsupport Colleges," *Educational and Psychological Measurement,* vol. 18, 1958, pp. 841–844; Gilmore, John V., "A New Venture in the Testing of Motivation," *College Board Review,* vol. 15, 1951, pp. 221–226; Kern, Donald W., "The Prediction of Academic Success of Freshmen in a Community College," *Dissertation Abstracts,* vol. 15, 1955, p. 85; Klugh, Henry E., and Robert Bierley, *op. cit.;* Melton, Richard S., "Differentiation of Successful and Unsuccessful Premedical Students," *Journal of Applied Psychology,* vol. 39, 1955, pp. 397–400; O'Neill, Ralph C., *op. cit.;* Parres, John, "Prediction of Academic Success in the Undergraduate Schools of the University of Pennsylvania," *Dissertation Abstracts,* vol. 15, 1955, pp. 2105–2106; Scannell, Dale P., *op. cit.;* Worell, Leonard, "Level of Aspiration and Academic Success," *Journal of Educational Psychology,* vol. 50, 1959, pp. 47–54.

14. Swensen, Clifford H., Jr., "College Performance of Students with High and Low High School Grades When Academic Aptitude Is Controlled," *Journal of Educational Research,* vol. 50, 1957, pp. 597–603.

15. Boyd, Joseph D., *op. cit.;* Franz, Gretchen, Junius Davis, and Dolores Garcia, *op. cit.;* Klugh, Henry E., and Robert Bierley, *op. cit.;* Scannell, Dale P., *op. cit.*

16. Horst, Paul, "Differential Prediction in College Admissions," *College Board Review,* vol. 33, 1957, pp. 19–23; Horst, Paul, *Differential Prediction of Academic Success,* University of Washington, Seattle, 1959 (mimeo.).

17. Horst, Paul, *Differential Prediction . . . , op. cit.*

18. Travers, Robert M. W., "Significant Research on the Prediction of Academic Success" in Donahue, W. T., and associates, editors, *The Measurement of Student Adjustment and Achievement.* University of Michigan Press, Ann Arbor, 1949.

19. Fisher, Joseph T., *op. cit.*

20. Anderson, Rodney Ebon, "The Use of Entrance Tests in the Differential Prediction of Freshman College Achievement, and the Effect of an Item Analysis on the Efficiency of the Predictive Batteries," *Dissertation Abstracts,* vol. 16, 1956, p. 2344.

21. Cronbach, Lee, J., *op. cit.*

22. Berdie, Ralph F., "Aptitude, Achievement, Interest, and Personality Tests: A Longitudinal Comparison," *Journal of Applied Psychology,* vol. 39, 1955, pp. 103–114.

23. Eells, Kenneth, "How Effective is Differential Prediction in Three Types of College Curricula?" *Educational and Psychological Measurement,* vol. 21, 1961, pp. 459–471.

24. Berdie, Ralph F., *op. cit.*

25. Berdie, Ralph F., "Intra-Individual Variability and Predictability," *Educational and Psychological Measurement,* vol. 21, 1961, pp. 663–676.

26. Forehand, G. A., Jr., and Louis C. McQuitty, "Configurations of Factor Standings as Predictors of Educational Achievement," *Educational and Psychological Measurement,* vol. 19, 1959, pp. 31–43.

27. Cronbach, Lee J., *op. cit.*

28. Travers, Robert M. W., *op. cit.*

29. Friedhoff, W. H., "Relationships Among Various Measures of Socio-economic Status, Social Class Identification, Intelligence, and School Achievement," *Dissertation Abstracts,* vol. 15, 1955, p. 2098; Gough, Harrison, "What Determines the Academic Achievement of High School Students?" *Journal of Educational Research,* vol. 46, 1953, pp. 321–331.

30. Carter, Harold D., "Improving the Prediction of School Achievement by Use of the California Study Methods Survey," *Educational Administration and Supervision,* vol. 45, 1959, pp. 255–260; Jacobs, James N., "Aptitude and Achievement Measures in Predicting High School Academic Success," *Personnel and Guidance Journal,* vol. 37, 1959, pp. 334–341.

31. Nason, Leslie J., *Academic Achievement of Gifted High School Students,* University of Southern California Press, Los Angeles, 1958, p. 92.

32. Jacobs, James N., *op. cit.;* Nason, Leslie J., *op. cit.*

33. Wellman, Frank E., "Differential Prediction of High School Achievement Using Single Score and Multiple Factor Tests of Mental Maturity," *Personnel and Guidance Journal,* vol. 35, 1957, pp. 512–517.

34. Mitchell, Blythe C., "The Relation of High School Achievement to the Abilities Measures by the Holzinger-Crowder Uni-Factor Test," *Educational and Psychological Measurement,* vol. 15, 1955, pp. 487–490.

35. Wolking, William D., "Predicting Academic Achievement with the Differential Aptitude and the Primary Mental Abilities Test," *Journal of Applied Psychology,* vol. 39, 1955, pp. 115–118.

36. Jacobs, James N., *op. cit.*

37. Hinkelman, Emmett A., "Relationship of Intelligence to Elementary School Achievement," *Educational Administration and Supervision,* vol. 41, 1955, pp. 176–179.

38. Barnes, Paul J., "Prediction of Achievement in Grades One Through Four from Otis Quick-Scoring Mental Ability Tests: Alpha Short Form," *Educational and Psychological Measurement,* vol. 15, 1955, pp. 493–494.

39. Further discussion of this finding is presented in Chapter 6.

Chapter 5

Personality Factors as Predictors

ALTHOUGH ABILITY MEASURES are presently the best single type of predictor, they account for less than half of the variation in academic performance. Thus, we are led to a consideration of nonintellective factors. In this connection, many investigators study academic performance by focusing upon personality characteristics as explanatory variables. This chapter reviews these studies and summarizes what is currently known about the role of such factors in academic performance.

The survey is organized around a listing of specific personality variables. In the literature these are usually selected through common sense or a hunch that they might be related to academic performance rather than on the basis of a systematic personality theory.

Some variables seem to refer to motivational states; these include anxiety, achievement motivation, level of interest in different content areas, and the like. A second type involves what might be termed personality "style." Illustrative are factors such as degree of independence, impulse control, and introversion. A third factor, which involves the cognitive level, is the self-concept. Still other factors, such as measures of study habits, seem to point more directly to the behavioral level. Finally, some studies focus upon manifestations of pathology to account for achievement. Examples are inventories of adjustment, such as the Minnesota Multiphasic Personality Inventory, and clinical instruments, such as the Rorschach.

Because the emphases in the literature are so eclectic, it is difficult to organize this review in terms of a systematic classification of personality factors. In fact, to do so would create a misleading sense of orderliness in the literature. For these reasons, we simply list the variables. At the close of the chapter, where an assessment is made of the current state of knowledge, at least a preliminary classification of factors will emerge.

The findings for each personality variable are reviewed according to a number of subcategories. Results are presented separately for each educational level, and sex differences are noted where they occur. Furthermore, the findings of studies in which ability is controlled are reported separately. This is done because, as noted in Chapter 2, the usefulness of any personality factor as a predictor cannot be evaluated unless it is shown to be independent of ability.

Two basic methods of analysis are used in the studies of personality variables. First, the correlational method is used to assess the degree of relationship between the personality factor and academic performance. In studies using this method ability is controlled either by means of partial correlation analysis or by multiple correlation in which the contribution of a personality variable to a battery of intellective factors is assessed. By the second technique performance is studied by composing groups of high and low achievers or under- and overachievers, and assessing possible personality differences between such groups. The terms "overachievement" and "underachievement" will be used only when the method of composing these groups corresponds to the requirements set forth in Chapter 2—that is, when there is a discrepancy between actual performance and predicted performance. When the method of composing groups results in failure to control ability, the terms "overachievement" and "underachievement" will not be used. Some studies misuse the over- and underachievement concepts; they control for intelligence, but use a technique of composing groups that really conforms to our definition of high and low achievement. When this is the case, we shall apply the latter terms.

Most of the studies to be reviewed assess the relationship between a single personality variable and academic performance. However, a few investigations use from 2 to more than 10 variables. Findings from these single-variable and multivariate approaches are reported under separate headings.

I. SINGLE-VARIABLE STUDIES

Measures of Study Habits and Attitudes Toward Study

Measures of study habits and attitudes are commonly used in prediction studies. Some measures simply assess the actual mechanics of studying; others tap the student's attitudes toward studying and/or schoolwork in general. Often, both study habits and attitudes are surveyed in a single inventory. Aside from these self-report, pencil-and-paper inventories, there are some studies which use teacher and peer ratings.

Assessments of Study Mechanics. Three investigations on the college level indicate that when ability is controlled, study habits are positively related to academic performance.[1] Similar findings were obtained in four other studies, but ability was not properly controlled.[2] One additional investigation found that amount of time spent in study was not a crucial factor in academic performance.[3]

These findings suggest that inventories which assess study mechanics are useful in the prediction of academic performance. They shed no light on the question of sex differences in study habits, however, because the investigations using mixed samples failed to separate the sexes.

On the high school level, one study methods inventory correlated significantly with grades when ability was controlled.[4] This study did not assess sex differences.

Assessments of Attitudes Toward School and Studying. Kerns found a tendency for overachievers to attend college for intellectual reasons and for underachievers to attend for "negative" reasons, such as getting away from home.[5] Birney and Taylor developed a measure of orientation to college which covered two general kinds of attitudes:[6] a social orientation to college (valuing making friends, having a good time) and a scholastic orientation to college (valuing intellectual pursuits). They found that for male college seniors the scholastic orientation correlated slightly (.29) with grades when ability was controlled. For freshmen, however, there was essentially no correlation between the inventory and grades. Another study found that at both the college and high school levels a positive attitude toward school and the opinion that education is valuable have a slight positive relation to academic performance.[7] However, in this study ability was not controlled.

Inventories of Study Habits and Study Attitudes. A frequently used measure for the assessment of both study habits and study attitudes is an inventory developed by Brown and Holtzman called the Survey of Study Habits and Attitudes (SSHA).[8] These investigators suggest that more important than *how* one studies may be the degree of effort and the kind of attitude brought to the study situation. They developed an original 188-item inventory in which some of the items referred to study attitudes dimensions and others referred to study mechanics dimensions. On a college population, the study attitudes items differentiated over- and underachievers more efficiently than did the study mechanics items. A refined scale was then validated and cross-validated on separate groups of men and women at 10 colleges. For both males and females, the mean correlation with grades was about .40. A multiple correlation of about .70 was obtained when the inventory and an ability measure were combined for the prediction of grades. The findings were presented separately for each sex, and no significant sex differences were observed.

Another report indicated that the SSHA independently accounts for some of the variation in grades in college.[9] Lum found that for three groups (overachievers, underachievers, and normal achievers) of female college students, the SSHA differentiated on some subscales but not on others.[10] In a study whose findings were contradictory to those cited above, Ahmann and associates observed that the inventory did not add significantly to a battery of intellective measures in predicting college grades.[11] Another study revealed that the SSHA did not differentiate probationary students from nonprobationers.[12]

Chahbazi used an inventory for the prediction of college grades.[13] This measure (Cornell Orientation Inventory) consists of study habits, motivational, and adjustment items. Its addition to a battery of intellective measures increased the multiple correlation only slightly, and further analysis indicated that only the study habits items differentiated over- and underachievers.

While the findings cited above are not clear-cut, the general trend suggests that combinations of study attitudes and study habits items are useful in predicting academic performance. However, the results do not establish the superiority of one or the other type of item.

Teacher and Peer Ratings of Study Habits. O'Leary found that with ability controlled there was a correlation of .63 between teacher ratings of the work habits of high school students and academic achievement.[14] In another study on the high school level, Norton used both teacher and peer ratings in an effort to assess whether these are better than ability in predicting grades in a general science course.[15] He found that teacher ratings of study habits are not more closely related to grades than are aptitudes. However, for boys, peer ratings were more closely associated with grades than were aptitudes, and teacher ratings were negatively associated. For boys, teacher and peer ratings were significantly different; while for girls there was no difference. These findings suggest that the classroom behavior of boys is not strongly related to their level of academic performance; whereas that of girls is more closely related. In addition, these findings suggest that the criteria used by girls in rating one another may be quite similar to the criteria used by the teacher in rating them; whereas boys used criteria in their peer ratings that were not used by the teacher. Of course, the reasons for the differential perception of the teacher and for the discrepancies between peer perceptions and teacher perceptions can be assessed only through additional research.

Summary and Evaluation. The body of research on study habits and attitudes can be summarized under a few points. First, measures of study habits can predict academic performance even where ability is controlled. In addition, the studies show that positive attitudes toward school, such as beliefs in the value of intellectual pursuit and of education in general, are positively related to academic performance. However, it is not possible to state whether study habits items are better predictors than study attitudes items. This question can be assessed only through more research.

Even though the general trend of the findings indicates the usefulness of these measures, there are a few inconsistent findings. More work is needed to assess the reasons for this variability. One possibility is that schools vary in their organizational structure and/or in the characteristics of the students, and that these factors interact in some way so as to affect the magnitude of the relations between study habits, attitudes toward school, and academic performance.

With regard to sex differences, the few studies which control this factor show that measures of study habits and attitudes are equally useful in predicting academic performance for either sex.

Research using teacher and peer ratings of study habits as predictors is quite scanty, but it suggests that such measures may have some association with performance. However, these positive findings may be spurious. For example, teachers may consider good study habits and attitudes to be a prerequisite for high grades. If this is the case, then high ratings on study habits would be assigned to higher-achieving students not only because they do, in fact, have good study habits, but also because the teacher may be rationalizing what he believes to be an important source of academic success. Thus, teacher ratings may well represent nothing more than post hoc explanations rather than predictions, and they may be determined mainly by the teacher's need to make facts fit into his own set of preexistent biases (that a student cannot be successful unless he studies hard). In short, ratings of this kind may not really be predictors, because they must be obtained on the basis of the teacher's experience with the student. They occur subsequent to the student's performance rather than prior to it, so that any causal significance attached to them is of dubious validity. However, such ratings might be useful in studies which use achievement tests as the criterion of academic performance and in which the teacher is ignorant of the test score at the time he makes the ratings.

Research on study habits and attitudes is underrepresented on the high school level and absent on the elementary school level.

Measures of Interest

Interest measures generally have been put to three uses for the prediction of academic performance. In the first, scores on particular interest categories have been related to performance in corresponding course work. It would be predicted, for example, that students with high scores on interest in science will have higher grades in science courses than students whose expressed interests in this area are low.

Another use attempts to assess whether interests of any type are predictive of academic performance. Illustrative would be a finding that artistic interests are related to performance.

A third concern is not with substantive interests, but with certain general dimensions which cut across content, such as the clarity of interests, their intensity, and the like. In this case, the researcher deals with such questions as whether students with definite vocational goals do better than students who remain uncommitted.

Substantive Interests and Performance in Corresponding Courses. Cronbach states that although they have low correlations with grades, substantive interest measures improve the predictions obtained by using ability measures alone.[16] He also states that specific keys of the Dunlap Academic Preference Blank predict grades in corresponding courses from .50 to .70. Travers found that interest tests were of some value for predicting grades in courses within the areas of interests.[17] In a study by Collins the school subjects section of the Strong Vocational Interest Blank correlated .19 with grade-point average.[18] Two studies used the physician key of the Strong for predicting grades of premedical students.[19] One of these, Hewer's study, found that when ability was controlled, there was little relationship between the physician key and grades of male freshmen, but there was some evidence that *differences* between grades in certain courses were related to the predictor. In the other study, by Melton, the physician scale was uncorrelated with academic performance. In a study of engineering students, interest test scores were unrelated to performance.[20]

Two conclusions are suggested by these college-level studies. First, it appears that for students enrolled in a professional curriculum, measures of interest are not related to performance. This is not surprising, since enrollment in a professional curriculum presupposes a high level of interest in the area. Thus, one would not expect interest in medicine to be correlated with performance in a premedical program, since the amount of variation in this interest is probably minimal. However, for students enrolled in nonspecialized curricula, the research suggests that interest measures are useful for predicting performance in parallel course areas.

The studies cited have been carried out either on samples of males or on combined samples where sex is not controlled. Because of this, it is not possible to assess the presence of sex differences.

On the high school level, Shepler observed that with ability controlled, interest in science is positively related to science accomplishment.[21] No studies of this type were found for the elementary school level.

General Assessments of Interests in Relation to Academic Performance. Of those studies that assess whether interests of any kind can predict performance, only one controlled adequately for ability. This study found that among college students, underachievers have stronger interests in social activities than in intellectual activities, and that the opposite is true for overachievers.[22] A similar finding was observed in another study, although in this case there was no control for ability.[23] Diener found that degree of artistic interests was negatively related to performance, but he did not control adequately for ability.[24]

On the high school level, one investigation found that interest in social activities was negatively related to performance. It fails to control adequately for ability, however.[25]

Abstract Dimensions of Interest. Rust and Ryan present data indicating that overachievers in college tend to have higher interest scores on high prestige occupations,[26] a finding that suggests that interest measures may be an index of social aspiration level.

Cronbach asserted that the intensity of interests as measured by the Strong test was directly related to grades.[27] This indicates that interest measures also may be tapping a motivational factor.

Six college-level studies have investigated clarity of vocational or educational choice as a predictor of scholastic performance.[28] These show that students who are more certain of their occupational choice or who have definitely chosen a major field of study are likely to perform at a higher level than students who are unsure of what goals they wish to pursue. Two of these studies do not adequately control for ability.[29]

Of the four studies in which ability is adequately controlled, two show the presence of a sex difference.[30] Choice of a major field is directly related to academic performance in the case of males, but no such relationship pertains for females. Perhaps the psychological significance of commitment to a major course of study is different for males than for females.

Another dimension which has received attention is whether students choose their own goals or goals set for them by others. For the college level, one study found that of a group of students admitted to college on probation, those who were successful in their school work were more likely to have set their own goals and that these goals were more often in line with their measured interests.[31] The findings of another study are contrary to those just noted.[32]

On the high school level, Armstrong found that underachievers differed from normally achieving students in that the former more often chose occupational goals set for them by others, and these goals were not in line with their interests as measured by standard tests.[33]

A novel approach in the use of interests has been developed by Edwards and Wilson.[34] They formulated a two-way classification of interests: on the one hand, there is what they call the preference for social versus nonsocial objects, and on the other, there is the preference for reaching ends through deliberation versus the preference for immediate ends. Using high school students, they found that students having a deliberative orientation toward social objects had higher grades in chemistry and physics. However, the sexes differed in that males tended to show a deliberative orientation toward nonsocial objects (they were more likely to find science courses more intrinsically interesting), while females were more likely to show the deliberative orientation toward the social environment (they were motivated by a need to obtain high grades rather than by intrinsic interest). While ability was not adequately controlled in this research, the novel approach deserves further investigation.

Summary and Evaluation. On the basis of those studies that control adequately for ability, measures of interest, both in terms of content and in terms of more abstract characteristics, are useful in predicting academic performance. With regard to sex differences, the evidence suggests that for females the clarity of interests is not related to academic performance. However, for substantive interest measures it is not possible to assess sex differences because these studies either do not control for sex or utilize samples of males only.

The research on interests is weak in several respects. First, although many studies have been carried out on the college level, comparable research on the high school and, especially, elementary school levels is scarce. Second, little attention has been paid to the control of sex differences. Finally, it is not at all clear that some of the dimensions that are called interests should really be included in this category. Traditionally, this term has been used with reference to whether or not one "likes" a specific subject matter. However, the meaning of other usages is less clear. Thus, if we observe that students differ according to their preference for social as against intellectual activities, preference for the former may be an index of the need for affiliation. To cite another example, where high achievers tend to have higher interest scores on high prestige occupations, this interest may well be an index of social mobility aspiration.

As we pointed out in Chapter 3, there are a large number of concepts used in studies of academic achievement, and the boundaries of meaning are not well delineated. One index of usefulness of a variable in this type of research is that it accounts independently for some of the variation in performance. It is not clear that the term "interest" in some of the senses in which it has been used is independent of other concepts.

In light of these considerations, future studies should assess the relationship of interest measures to other concepts such as need for affiliation and mobility aspirations. In this way, we may be able to make more definitive judgments concerning the independent utility of the interest construct.

Measures of Achievement Motivation

The concept of achievement motivation refers to the need of an individual to perform according to a high standard of excellence. It has been measured in two general ways: by projective techniques and by pencil-and-paper questionnaires. Illustrative of the former is McClelland's method in which a subject is presented with a series of pictures and asked to compose a story in response to each of them.[35] The stories are scored in terms of the frequency with which achievement themes appear. This method is exemplified by the Thematic Apperception Test. The picture cards presented to the subject are referred to as TAT cards.

The research findings are presented under three headings: first are findings obtained through the use of projective measures; second are findings obtained through the use of questionnaires; and third is an assessment of the comparative usefulness of these two types of measures.

Projective Measures of Need for Achievement. We cite 12 relevant studies using projective techniques—9 on the college level, 2 on the high school level, and 1 on a graduate professional school sample. Of the 9 college studies, 4 found positive relations between achievement motivation and academic performance. All 9 controlled adequately for ability. McClelland and associates found that for a sample of male students, the correlation between grades and achievement motivation, as measured by the TAT, was .39.[36] In another study the TAT measure correlated .34 with grades, aptitude correlated at .55, and together these measures produced a multiple correlation of .63.[37] Burgess found that overachievers were significantly higher on need for achievement than underachievers.[38] Chahbazi used two projective measures scored for achievement motivation, and found that when these were added to a battery of six tests, the multiple correlation of the battery with college grades increased from .51 to .63.[39] The first three studies cited above were conducted using all-male samples; the fourth does not state the sex composition of the sample.

Five of the college studies showed projective measures of achievement motivation to be unrelated to performance. Walter used a special pictorial projective test for measuring achievement motivation in an attempt to assess its relation to the learning of certain study skills.[40] Achievement motivation was related to only one of five performance criteria. Another study found achievement motivation to be unrelated to any performance criteria.[41] The negative results were attributed in part to the low reliability of the TAT. In this connection a third investigation found that test-retest reliabilities of the TAT were quite low (about .25).[42] A fourth study used two groups of males of differing achievement levels and found that the TAT measure of achievement motivation did not differentiate between them.[43] Mitchell, using a sample of females in a teacher training curriculum, found the TAT to be unrelated to grades.[44] However, his control for ability was inadequate.

On the high school level, Rosen found that a TAT measure of achievement motivation was directly related to school grades for a sample of males. However, he failed to control for intelligence.[45]

Hills, in a study of first-year law school students, used six TAT cards for the measurement of general achievement motivation and three cards each for the measurement of achievement motivation on four specific levels (economic, social, academic, and professional).[46] He found that these various TAT scores correlated neither with each other nor with several criteria of academic success, including grades. These findings could be attributed to the unreliability of the measures, or to the homogeneity of law school samples with regard to achievement motivation, or to both of these factors.

Questionnaire Measures of Achievement Motivation. Studies using questionnaire measures of achievement motivation present a clearer overall picture than do the projective measures. At the college level, six investigations found positive relations between achievement motivation and academic performance. Three used the need achievement scale from the Edwards Personal Preference Schedule.[47] In all of these ability was controlled adequately. The other three used a measure of level of aspiration as an index of achievement motivation.[48] However, in one ability was not properly controlled.[49] All six either used male samples or did not state the findings separately by sex.

One high-school-level study found a positive relation between aspiration level and academic achievement.[50] In this study the method of controlling ability was inadequate.

Hills observed low but significant correlations (.30) between questionnaire tests of achievement motivation and some criteria of academic success in law school, although no significant relation with grades was found.[51]

Comparative Assessment of Projective and Questionnaire Measures. A few studies use both projective and pencil-and-paper measures of achievement motivation. In a study by Weiss and associates in which achievement motivation was measured by both the TAT and the achievement scale of the Edwards Personal Preference Schedule, the latter showed a higher zero-order correlation with grades; however, when each was separately combined with an aptitude measure, there was little difference in the two multiple correlations.[52] In addition, these two measures showed little association with each other (a correlation of only .26). Melikian also found no association between these two measures.[53] In the study by Hills, TAT measures correlated neither with themselves nor with any criteria of academic success; while questionnaire measures showed significant correlations with some criteria of academic success.[54]

Mitchell administered eight measures of achievement motivation to a sample of college females.[55] Two were projective measures—the TAT and a sentence-completion test. The eight measures were factor analyzed, and six factors were isolated: (1) academic motivation and efficiency; (2) self-satisfaction; (3) wish-fulfillment motivation (strong achievement desire with little application in behavior); (4) nonacademic achievement orientation; (5) external pressure to achieve (such as parental pressures); (6) a factor similar to 3 above. Grade-point average was related only to factor 1. Ability was not adequately controlled, however. The projective sentence-completion test was related to factors 3 and 6. The TAT measure did not load highly on any factor, probably a result of unreliability. Despite the fact that ability was not adequately controlled, this investigation is significant because it strongly indicates that achievement motivation is not a unitary concept. It shows that achievement motivation consists of a number of dimensions represented by the factors described above. Moreover, it suggests that only one specific dimension of achievement motivation is related to academic performance and that objective measures seem to tap this dimension better than projective tests. Furthermore, the evidence suggests that projective tests measure a wish-fulfillment dimension of achievement motivation that is not related to performance criteria. Of course, this study needs replication under conditions where ability is adequately controlled. It should also be carried out on male samples and at different educational levels.

Summary and Evaluation. We find that the results of studies using projective measures of achievement motivation are very inconsistent. Some studies have found projective measures to be positively related to performance, while others have found no relationship. One factor possibly contributing to the inconsistency in these findings is the low reliability of projective measures, particularly the TAT.[56]

Questionnaire measures of achievement motivation provide consistent and positive relations with academic performance though these relationships are not very strong. On the basis of their greater consistency, these questionnaire measures seem at present to be more useful than the projective measures.

These studies offer no basis for a generalization regarding sex differences in the relationship of achievement motivation to academic performance. Moreover, studies on the high school level are infrequent, and no studies on the elementary school level have been found for this variable. Additional research is needed to eliminate these deficiencies.

In general, the research does not indicate that achievement motivation is strikingly related to academic performance. On the face of it, such a variable would be expected to exhibit stronger relations with performance criteria. We need to consider why this is not the case.

Aside from technical reasons such as low reliability, there may be some relevant theoretical points. One question involves the conceptual status of the achievement motivation construct. Mitchell's work shows that it is a multidimensional concept.[57] It may have greater predictive usefulness when the dimensions most relevant to academic performance are specified. More studies in this direction are needed.

Another important problem is related to the assumption made by many researchers that achievement motivation scores can be used directly to predict academic achievement. This may be an oversimplified approach. Other variables may operate concurrently with achievement motivation or as mediating factors to suppress or sometimes to accentuate its relations with academic performance. That is, achievement motivation may be directly related to performance for some individuals, inversely related for others, and unrelated for still others, depending upon the differential operation of additional factors.

For example, some persons who are high on achievement motivation may also be high on fear of failure. That is, while they aspire to a high level of performance, they may be afraid that they will be unable to reach this level. This anxiety may interfere with actual performance.[58] Under these conditions, a measure of achievement motivation probably would not correlate very highly with performance—not because it is unrelated to performance, but because of the operation of a mediating factor. More work directed to the discovery of such factors is needed. The crucial point is that the use of isolated personality characteristics may not always be a fruitful procedure. The effect of additional characteristics on any one of interest as a predictor must be assessed.

In short, future research on achievement motivation must address itself first to the isolation of the specific dimensions of this variable, second to the assessment of those dimensions most clearly related to academic performance, and third to the specification of other variables which may mediate the relation of achievement motivation to academic performance.

Measures of Independence

Measures of independence show some promise of being useful predictors of academic performance. Conceptually, this variable has been used in different senses. It sometimes refers to the need to make decisions and select alternative courses of action on one's own without seeking the advice or support of others. Items which characteristically differentiate independent from nonindependent subjects are, for example, the following: "plans alone without suggestions or discussion"; "usually faces troubles alone without seeking help"; "prefers to work things out his own way rather than accept suggestions."[59] The concept also has been used in the sense of conformity to or deviation from some group norm. Sometimes, terms such as "self-sufficiency" or "autonomy" are used synonymously with independence.

Findings. Independence appears to be positively related to academic performance. Weigand found that among two groups of freshmen admitted to college on probation, those who were removed from probation were more likely to have chosen their goals independently of the influence of others.[60] Burgess reported that underachieving engineering students were higher on need for dependency as measured by the TAT than their overachieving counterparts.[61] Another study found that higher-achieving students were more independent than low achievers, but aptitude was not controlled.[62]

In a study of the relation of personality factors to performance on an examination under conditions of manipulated stress, Carrier found that male students with a tendency toward dependence on others in decision-making were more negatively affected by stress than were more independent students.[63] Merrill and Murphy classified a group of low-ability college students according to whether they performed better than predicted on the basis of ability and thus remained in college or whether they were failing as expected.[64] Using the Edwards Personal Preference Schedule, they found that the group that was not failing was higher on the autonomy scale.

Erb took a sample of college students who fell just above and just below the median on ability (in order to control this factor) and divided it into groups high and low on conformity.[65] He defined high conformity as the production of responses on a Q-sort which were modal for the group, and low conformity as the production of atypical responses. For females, conformity and grade-point average were directly related. For males, conformity was unrelated to performance.

Summary and Evaluation. The findings suggest that independence tends to be positively related to academic performance. However, certain questions remain unanswered. First, some evidence suggests that independence measures may be correlated with the concept of achievement motivation. Thus, a study by Douvan and Adelson indicates that boys with upwardly mobile aspirations showed more autonomy on a series of interview items, suggesting that achievement motivation and independence are related.[66] This conclusion is supported by McClelland and associates who reported that when TAT protocols from the Asch experiment were scored, 13 of 15 nonyielders (independents) were above the median in achievement motivation, while 13 of 15 yielders were below the median.[67] Also relevant is a study by Young in which it was hypothesized that achievement motivation will vary directly with independence, where independence was defined as degree of parental training for self-decision-making.[68] The relationship of the two variables was in the predicted direction, although it fell just short of a statistically significant level.

Thus, independence may be a part of a larger constellation of variables that define a general achievement orientation. Further research is needed, therefore, to establish the extent to which this measure accounts independently for variation in academic performance.

All of the studies cited have been carried out on the college level. Research on the lower levels is needed. Moreover, very little attention has been given to sex differences in these studies. With only one exception, all used samples of males or pooled samples in which sex was not controlled.

Measures of Impulsivity

Parsons has pointed out that in a universalistic, achievement-oriented society, adequate adult role performance often requires delay in immediate gratifications in the interest of long-run goals.[69] The intellectual requirements of the educational process furnish a specific example of this. The ability to delay immediate gratification and to persist at tasks when the rewards lie in the future is certainly a requirement of the student educational role. Thus, variations in this personality characteristic are expected to be related to academic performance.

A number of different terms used in research seem to be variants of the impulse control concept. These include persistence, endurance, and compulsiveness. The last-mentioned term probably is not usually considered to be similar to impulse control, since it has connotations of maladaptive rigidity and inflexibility that impulse control does not have. However, within a given role context such as the student role, it might often be impossible to distinguish between behavior indicative of persistence and behavior indicative of compulsiveness. To distinguish between the two probably requires analysis on the psychodynamic level rather than on the behavioral level.

The Findings. Five studies relevant to impulsivity have been made on the college level. Merrill and Murphy found that for a sample of low-ability students, the endurance scale of the Edwards Personal Preference Schedule differentiated between those compiling successful and unsuccessful academic records.[70] This same scale differentiated over- and underachievers in a study of freshmen engineering students.[71] Weigand's study of probationary students found that the successful students were able to persist toward their objectives in the face of adversities, while the unsuccessful ones were not.[72]

Two other studies show that interest test scores may be better predictors of academic performance for noncompulsive than for compulsive students.[73] The accounting scale of the Strong Vocational Interest Blank was used as a measure of compulsiveness, apparently on the assumption that interest in accounting is an index of this general trait. When a group of engineering students were classified according to whether they were high or low on compulsiveness, interest measures correlated more highly with grades for the noncompulsive students. The rationale here was that compulsives will tend to work hard regardless of whether they have much interest in particular courses, while noncompulsives will put forth variable effort depending upon the direction of their interests. Thus, interest scores will be better predictors for the latter. Unfortunately, this study does not establish that compulsives and noncompulsives are equivalent in ability. Nevertheless, the findings are of interest because they provide a concrete illustration of the general point that the predictive usefulness of one personality factor may be affected by the operation of another personality factor. In the present case the predictive utility of interest measures may be affected by the degree of compulsiveness.

On the high school level MacArthur factor analyzed a number of persistence measures and found that an eight-test battery defining a general persistence factor correlated about .25 with school achievement.[74] Another study on the high school level by McDavid attempted to apply some of the work of Schroder and Hunt to the prediction of academic performance.[75] The latter studied responses to problem-solving situations under conditions of induced failure or criticism. One kind of response to this situation was called "failure avoidance." Two types of avoidance were observed: failure avoidance *behavior,* defined as withdrawal from the task situation; and failure avoidance *interpretation,* defined as a refusal to perceive personal inadequacy under the negative conditions. McDavid assumed that grades are a form of approval or disapproval and that therefore students differing in performance level should differ in the kinds of self-evaluation they make. Self-evaluation was measured by a test designed to assess the kinds of reactions students have to approval or disapproval. The findings suggested that higher-achieving students respond to high grades with increased incentive and that the lower-achievers respond to lower grades with decreased incentive. Thus, persistence is here viewed as a variable dependent on performance with a feedback effect which tends to affect future performance. That is, high grades result in a higher level of persistence, which in turn may lead to higher grades; while low grades may produce the opposite effect. Unfortunately in this case the method of defining performance groups may have resulted in failure to control for ability. Nevertheless the approach certainly deserves further investigation because it suggests that certain personality variables may be results of—as well as determinants of—academic performance.

Summary and Evaluation. The preceding studies indicate that impulse control is positively related to performance. Sex differences were not examined. Whether impulse control is related to performance independently of other variables such as achievement motivation remains an open question. One study indicated that upward-aspiring boys show greater internalization of personal standards, and the items on which this conclusion was based seem to resemble what has been referred to here as impulse control.[76] Thus, additional research is required to establish that this variable can independently account for variation in academic performance.

Measures of Anxiety

Research assessing the effects of anxiety upon level of academic performance is of three general types. The first examines the role of general anxiety, frequently using the Taylor Manifest Anxiety Scale (MAS). The second uses measures of anxiety in such specific situations as test-taking. And the third focuses on both kinds of measures, assessing the relations between the two and comparing their efficiency in predicting performance.

The Role of General Anxiety. Seven studies using general anxiety measures on the college level have been reviewed;[77] of these, only three control adequately for ability.[78] We deal first with the latter studies. Spielberger and Katzenmeyer assessed the relationship between the MAS and grades for a sample of males divided into high, medium, and low ability groupings. The MAS had a low (−.18) negative correlation with grade-point average for subjects in the medium ability group, but was uncorrelated with grades for the other ability groups. In another study the MAS was uncorrelated with grades and with a measure of ability.[79] However, when the MAS was included in a predictive test battery, it added significantly to the multiple correlation. This was interpreted as an indication that the MAS apparently increases the validity of the battery by suppressing some of the grade-irrelevant variation in the other predictors. A third study found that anxiety enhances the predictability of grades from a knowledge of ability, but this holds mainly for subjects having high levels of anxiety.[80] That is, for highly anxious subjects the correlation between intelligence and grades is increased over what it would be if anxiety were not taken into account.

The college-level studies which did not control for intelligence produced inconsistent findings. Two found little relationship between the MAS and academic performance.[81] Another found that for a sample of females anxiety was positively related to performance, but a fourth investigation found it negatively related.[82]

On the elementary school level, Reese studied fourth- and sixth-grade males and females and found that anxiety, as measured by the children's Manifest Anxiety Scale, was negatively related to scores on an achievement test in mathematics.[83] However, when the MAS was added to a battery with an intelligence measure, the multiple correlation was not increased much beyond the level obtained using intelligence as the sole predictor. Another study attempted to assess the effects of age on the relation between anxiety and achievement.[84] For fifth-grade girls, high achievers showed more anxiety on the children's MAS than low achievers. But for sixth-grade girls, this relation was reversed. For boys no age difference was observed. While ability was not controlled in this study, the findings are worth noting because they suggest that in elementary school the effects of personality characteristics are unstable. Thus, it is important to conduct longitudinal studies in which personality is assessed repeatedly.

The Role of Situation-Specific Anxiety. The studies using more specific measures have been concerned with anxiety in test-taking situations. On the college level, Carrier investigated the relationship between personality characteristics and performance on course examinations under conditions of manipulated stress.[85] Four characteristics were studied: (1) permeability, or the tendency to be influenced by internal and external stimuli; (2) stability, or the degree of nervous tension; (3) achievement motivation; (4) need for affiliation, or the need to establish and/ or maintain affective relationships. It was found that those males who were high on permeability and those who were low on stability were more likely to be negatively affected under stress in the examination situation. One sex difference was noted—that females are more likely to be affected by induced stress than males.

In another study, college students were assigned to testing conditions that varied in the degree of anxiety, the types of testing instructions given, and the instructor who gave them.[86] When the instructions were not intended to reduce anxiety, low-anxious students performed better than high-anxious students, but when the instructions were intended to reduce anxiety, the high-anxious students outperformed the low-anxious students. Since intelligence was not controlled in this study, it is difficult to interpret these findings. Sarason found that test anxiety had low, negative correlations with both aptitude and grades, but the correlations with aptitude were higher than the correlations with grades.[87]

On the high school level, one study isolated a number of specific dimensions of anxiety and related these to various criteria of school performance.[88] Two of the anxiety dimensions were anxious hostility toward school and anxious hostility toward age-mates. These factors were related to school grades. A sex difference appeared in that these factors were more closely associated with grades for females than for males.

On the elementary school level, a study of British children found that test anxiety was unrelated to test performance.[89]

Comparison of General and Specific Anxiety Measures. Sarason used a college sample to investigate whether test anxiety is independent of more general anxiety as measured by the MAS.[90] He found that a measure of test anxiety is partly independent of more general measures (correlations are .41 for males and .49 for females) and that test anxiety has low negative correlations (about .15) with academic performance. However, the correlations are somewhat higher for women than for men. The MAS was not significantly related to performance. Ability was not controlled, and the relationship between test anxiety and grades might have disappeared if it had been.

An excellent study on this topic was conducted by Alpert and Haber.[91] Their research had three aims: first, to assess the relation of general anxiety scales such as the MAS to specific anxiety measures and to compare their relative efficiency in predicting grades; second, to determine the relation of anxiety to aptitude; and third, to explore the effects of the direction of anxiety upon performance. That is, they wanted to know whether a distinction between "facilitating" and "debilitating" anxiety would be useful for predicting academic performance. Using a sample of college males, they found that general anxiety measures are not highly related to specific test anxiety scales. In addition, they observed that specific anxiety measures are superior to general tests in the prediction of academic performance. Furthermore, general scales were independent of verbal aptitude, while specific tests were correlated with aptitude. However, in spite of this association, the specific tests accounted independently for some of the variation in grades. Thus, correlations of grade-point average and aptitude ranged from .27 to .43, while correlations between grades and a battery composed of aptitude plus specific anxiety measures ranged from .29 to .58. When test anxiety was differentiated into facilitating and debilitating types, each accounted independently for some of the variation in performance. This last finding suggests that the relationship of anxiety to academic performance may be nonlinear. That is, extremely low anxiety may be an indirect index of a very low level of achievement motivation, while moderate anxiety may indicate a higher level of achievement motivation and thus facilitate higher levels of academic performance. On the other hand, if anxiety were to reach a high level, it would begin to interfere with academic performance. If this were the case, the relationship between anxiety and academic performance would be curvilinear.

Summary and Evaluation. We have found that on the college level general measures of anxiety are not directly useful for the prediction of academic performance. However, some evidence does suggest that general anxiety may be useful in multiple correlation analyses, since it may boost the level of correlations between ability and grades. Research on elementary school children has been infrequent and what findings there are do not suggest that general anxiety is a useful predictor at this level.

The specific measures of test-taking anxiety, on the other hand, have produced somewhat more consistent results for college students. The findings suggest that test-taking anxiety has small negative relations with performance. The one study reviewed on high school students is also consistent with this trend.

A few sex comparisons are also to be noted. On the college level, there is no clear evidence of consistent sex differences in the relation between anxiety and performance, although one study suggests that anxiety has a stronger negative effect for females than for males. On the high school level one study suggests that anxieties about school and about age-mates have a stronger negative effect on academic performance for females than for males. Some evidence on the elementary school level indicates that the relationship between anxiety and performance changes through time in the case of girls but not in the case of boys.

We now consider some of the possible reasons for the inconsistency and the generally low relationships found between anxiety and academic performance. First, it may be that measures of anxiety are not being used correctly. Thus, while anxiety may be related to performance in a curvilinear fashion, the studies have not attempted to assess this possibility. Consideration of this point might remove many inconsistencies in the findings. In addition, the research exhibits little concern with possible relationships between anxiety and other concepts that may be related to it—such as achievement motivation, fear of failure, and the like. For example, achievement motivation may be highly related to academic performance at moderate levels of anxiety but not at high levels of anxiety. This suggests that the role of the anxiety concept is defined best not as a direct predictor of academic performance, but rather as a variable that sometimes accentuates or sometimes lowers the predictive utility of other personality variables.

In addition, the causal status of the concept needs clarification. We do not know whether the relations found between anxiety and performance indicate that anxiety leads to decrements in performance, whether poor past performance tends to increase anxiety about subsequent school performance, or whether both of these factors are operative. In short, anxiety and performance may be involved in a feedback relationship.

While it is certain that anxiety is not a unidimensional concept, the number and types of relevant dimensions are at present not well delineated. The literature has pointed to one variation—namely, the level of generality of anxiety (general anxiety as against test-taking anxiety)—but additional dimensions are probably involved. For example, one of the studies indicates that anxiety about social relationships with peers may affect school performance.[92] More work aimed at discovering the dimensions of the anxiety concept is needed.

Measures of Introversion

Several studies have explored the relation between introversion and academic performance. The term "introversion" refers to shyness and a tendency to withdraw from social contact; its opposite, extroversion, refers to a tendency toward sociability and the seeking of social contacts.

The Findings. Travers states that small positive relations have been found between the degree of introversion and academic success.[93] More recent research lends support to this conclusion, although most of it occurs on the college level. Bloomberg found that college students showing high academic performance are somewhat more introverted than students with lower perform-ance.[94] Another study found that underachievers derive their greatest pleasure in college from social activities while over-achievers derive their pleasure from academic activities.[95] Bir-ney and Taylor developed a measure of orientation to college covering two general areas: the social area (that is, the value of making friends and having a good time) and the scholastic area (that is, the value of education and intellectual pursuit).[96] For a sample of male college freshmen and seniors, these two orienta-tions were negatively associated. For freshmen neither orienta-tion was related to grades. For seniors the scholastic orientation correlated at .29 with grades when ability was controlled. In an-other study, Krug reported that among freshmen engineering students, overachievers were significantly lower than under-achievers on the need for affiliation scale of the Edwards Personal Preference Schedule.[97] A second study using the Edwards meas-ure came to a similar conclusion.[98] When Merrill and Murphy used the Edwards instrument to assess the personality character-istics of two groups of low-ability college students,[99] the group that performed better than predicted and remained in college was lower on need for affiliation than the group that was failing as ex-pected.

Beach studied the relation between sociability and academic performance in four different kinds of classroom situations.[100] These were lecture groups, discussion groups with an instructor, leaderless discussion groups, and independent study groups. Beach found that sociability was negatively related to achievement in the lecture and instructor-led discussion situations, positively re-lated in the leaderless groups, and unrelated in the independent study groups. These findings suggest that personality character-istics may interact in some way with characteristics of the class-room situation so as to produce higher or lower levels of aca-demic performance.

In a study by Knaak high-achieving female college students were lower on sociability than low-achieving ones.[101] However, this study, unlike the ones cited above, failed to control for ability.

One study on the high school level found low achievers to be more interested in social relationships than high achievers.[102] This investigation did not control adequately for intelligence.

Summary and Evaluation. These findings clearly suggest that introversion is positively related to academic performance. However, this generalization is good only for the college level, since research on other levels is practically nonexistent. In addition, no comparisons by sex were made in the studies that controlled adequately for ability.

While the findings are consistent, their theoretical significance is not obvious. One possible interpretation is that extroverts, in contrast to introverts, have less time to study because they are more preoccupied with social activities. On the other hand, the relationship may be more complex, involving the student's value system regarding the importance of academic work and the degree to which holding a particular value position on this issue is related to sociometric position within the student culture. That is, some students may appear to be introverted because they value intellectual pursuits to a degree which violates peer group norms (the "gentleman's C"); thus their value system forces them to sacrifice their social standing in the group and decreases the frequency and breadth of their social contacts. If this were the case, we should expect to find that introversion would be positively related to measures of independence. Further research is needed to assess possible relationships between introversion and independence.

Measures of the Self-Image

Historically, the behavioral sciences have devoted considerable attention on a theoretical level to the concept of the self, as exemplified in the work of Cooley, Mead, Cottrell, and Sullivan.[103] During the last few years some basic research has begun to accumulate, part of which has been conducted in connection with studies of academic performance.

The most visible theme running through the studies is a concern with the positive or negative aspect of the self-image. The terms used and the measures involved, however, show wide variation. Specifically, terms such as self-acceptance, positive self-image, self-esteem, and self-confidence seem to reflect a concern with a positive-negative continuum. A few other dimensions of the self-image are also used. For example, some studies deal with self-insight and the relative salience of self-characteristics.

The Findings. We review first studies on the college level. Brim found that students with high self-estimates of intelligence had higher grade-point averages than students of equal measured intelligence, but lower self-estimates of intelligence.[104] A study by Lum showed that among female college students, overachievers exhibited greater self-confidence than underachievers.[105] Stevens investigated the relationship between the self-image and academic achievement for a sample of bright college students.[106] He found that high achievers exhibited greater self-insight regarding their intellectual abilities and showed greater self-acceptance or positive attitude toward themselves; in addition, their achievement-related personality characteristics had greater salience. However, in this study the high and low achievers could have differed significantly in intelligence.

On the high school level, one study assessed the self-images of highly intelligent students who differed in level of achievement. Students were compared on a 200-item adjective checklist.[107] For boys, 13 adjectives differentiated, and for girls, there were 17 such adjectives. For the boys a higher achievement level was associated with a more positive self-image. The differentiating adjectives seemed in general to be directly related to academic work ("intelligent," "reliable," "clear-thinking," "realistic"). For girls a higher achievement level was not related to a more positive self-image, and the differentiating items were less relevant to academic work ("soft-hearted," "lovable").

In a study by McDavid it was hypothesized that high achievers have higher self-evaluations than low achievers.[108] This was found to be the case for a sample of boys. The method of picking achievement groups failed to control for intelligence, however. In spite of this shortcoming, the study is of interest, since the author suggests that this dimension of the self-image may operate as a feedback mechanism. That is, high academic performance may result in higher self-evaluation which, in turn, may increase the motivation for attaining high grades in the future.

Using a sample of elementary school children, Reeder found that students with low self-esteem have lower grades than students with higher self-esteem.[109]

Summary and Evaluation. Although research findings below the college level are spotty, the studies suggest that a positive self-image is associated with higher performance. The findings do not allow an assessment of sex differences in these relationships, because there have been practically no attempts to consider this question. However, one study suggests that the self-image characteristics differentiating high- and low-achieving females are different in content from those differentiating high- and low-achieving males.

These studies raise a number of issues requiring further research. One issue involves differences in measurement techniques. Sometimes self-image is assessed by computing discrepancies between ideal and actual evaluations provided by the subject; at other times the subject is asked to check whether certain qualities apply to him or to what extent he likes himself. Further studies are needed of the comparability of different operational procedures.

Another question is whether there are other dimensions of the self-image that are relevant to academic performance. Two possibilities are the stability and the generality of the self-image. The former refers to the degree to which the image is affected by the responses of others. That is, does disapproval immediately result in a negative self-evaluation, or is an original positive evaluation maintained in spite of this? Schroder and Hunt have done research suggesting that there are a variety of responses to negative evaluations from others and that these responses may have an effect upon future performance in problem-solving situations.[110] The implications of research by Bendig and Gluck are similar.[111]

The dimension of generality refers to the consistency of the self-image across different social situations—that is, whether the self-image varies or remains the same from one situation to another. For example, one might ask whether an individual has a positive self-evaluation in some academic areas but a negative evaluation in others. Then one could assess the degree to which variability of the self-image was related to differential performance in various subject areas.

A third issue concerns why certain kinds of self-images are related to level of academic performance. An example is Brim's finding that among persons of equivalent measured intelligence, those with the higher self-estimate will outperform those with the lower estimate. This could mean that the image of self is what is presented in interaction with others and what others respond to and make judgments about. Thus, the student who thinks he is not very intelligent may participate less in class discussion, may be inclined to give up sooner when working on difficult problems, and so forth. If this is the case, others may respond to him as if he were less bright than he is in fact, and this might result in a lower grade. This interpretation suggests the possibility of a relationship between the self-image and achievement motivation. In a study dealing with this, Martire found a positive relationship between the level of achievement motivation and the amount of discrepancy between ratings of the ideal and actual self on achievement-related traits.[112] That is, the higher the achievement motivation, the greater the discrepancy between what a subject wishes to be like and what he thinks he is like. Such evidence suggests that dimensions of the self-image concept are related to other variables that are relevant to academic performance. Further research is needed to map the relations between the self-image and other predictor variables.

A final issue concerns the causal role of self-image in academic performance. The studies do not establish whether the self-image is determined by prior performance or whether performance is determined by the self-image. One study on high school students was concerned with assessing changes in self-estimates of abilities from the ninth to the twelfth grade.[113] When self-estimates were compared with performance on objective ability tests, it was found that the congruence between the two was greater for the seniors than for the freshmen. This suggests that students use academic experience to revise their self-conception. But in all likelihood, self-image characteristics cannot be viewed exclusively as either determinants or results of social experience. Rather, the self-image is probably acquired in social situations and also helps to determine the course of future experience. However, because the self-image may be so sensitive to prior experience, it is of the utmost importance that its measurement precede the measurement of academic performance. Otherwise, it would be impossible to use measures of self-image as predictors having causal significance.

Measures of Adjustment

A number of investigations have studied the relationship between adjustment and academic performance, using the Minnesota Multiphasic Personality Inventory (MMPI) as the measure of adjustment. The MMPI is a clinically oriented instrument that defines a number of personality dimensions having pathological significance. All of the studies to be reviewed here were made on the college level.

The Findings. A few studies indicate that the MMPI is predictive of academic performance. Hackett isolated all items discriminating high and low achievers.[114] On a cross-validation sample, these items correlated .61 with grade-point average. A measure of ability correlated .39 with grade-point average and only .10 with the MMPI items. The two measures combined produced a multiple correlation of .69 with grades. Analysis of the items indicated that low achievers, unlike high achievers, were emotionally labile, defensive about revealing weakness, admired strength and power, and lacked warmth and acceptance of others. Jensen investigated the personality correlates of academic performance at different ability levels for a group of freshmen students.[115] The data showed that for a low-ability group, low achievers were higher than achievers on the schizophrenia, hypomania, and fake scales.

Seven studies have found that the MMPI is not related to academic performance. Burgess used a sample of males and found the MMPI to be unrelated to performance.[116] Two studies of a sample of college women obtained a multiple correlation of .64 with grades, using the MMPI and an ability measure as predictors.[117] However, on a second sample, this correlation dropped to .54, and the ability measure alone correlated at .50 with grades, indicating that the shrinkage occurred mainly in the MMPI. Quinn reported that MMPI items were unrelated to academic performance when ability was controlled.[118] Similar findings were obtained in a fifth study.[119] Studies by Clark and by Stone and Ganung also show the MMPI to be unrelated to performance.[120] Clark found that items differentiating over- and under-achievers in one sample failed to do so on a second sample. Stone and Ganung found that normal and maladjusted groups of female students were only slightly different in grade-point average, but they did not control for intelligence.

The MMPI has also been used in the form of profile patterns rather than scores on particular scales. Using male college freshmen, Hoyt and Norman attempted to test whether the correlation between grades and ability is higher for students with "normal" profiles than for students with "maladjusted" profiles.[121] They reasoned that maladjustment will lower the association between performance and ability because it produces either over- or underachievement. The data supported their hypothesis. However, no differences were found in the percentages of higher- and lower-achieving students scoring high or low on any specific MMPI scale. That is, while general maladjustment is related to academic performance, particular types of personality problems are not.

Drake and Oetting found that particular profiles were related to academic performance,[122] but they did not adequately control for aptitude.

Summary and Evaluation. This review shows that more often than not studies find the MMPI to be unrelated to academic performance. However, the study by Hoyt and Norman suggests that even though particular scales may not be related to performance, the presence of some type of maladjustment, as indicated by profile analysis, is likely to be associated with differences in achievement. Further research of this type seems warranted.

The Rorschach as a Predictor

The Rorschach Test, a projective instrument used most frequently in clinical work, provides a method of inferring underlying personality dynamics from the assessment of a number of dimensions of perceptual behavior. These dimensions have sometimes been used for predicting academic performance.

The Findings. All of the research to be cited has been carried out at the college level. In his review of the research Travers states that some Rorschach dimensions (such as receptivity to outer stimuli) are related to academic performance.[123] However, more recent research does not indicate that the Rorschach is a useful measure. Studies by Burgess, Clark, Cooper, Rust and Ryan, and Sopchak all find that the test predicts either poorly or not at all.[124] One study using the Rorschach on a group of highly intelligent students observed differences suggesting that the higher-achieving students were better adjusted.[125]

The Rorschach has been somewhat successful in distinguishing between groups of students who differ on performance criteria other than grades. One study found that Rorschach protocols were related to academic honors and extracurricular honors for a group of college girls.[126] McArthur and King found that students who have personal and social difficulties can be distinguished from a group of randomly chosen students on the basis of Rorschach response patterns.[127]

Summary and Evaluation. On the basis of these results, it seems that the Rorschach Test is a poor instrument for the prediction of academic performance. However, some of the findings suggest that it might be useful for predicting criteria other than grades.

Miscellaneous Personality Characteristics as Predictors

There is a scattering of research on a variety of other personality characteristics. In most cases only a few studies have been carried out on a given characteristic. Several of these studies seem promising.

Measures of Cognitive Style. Research by Gulliksen and associates suggests that the ability to make consistent judgments in paired comparison choices is related to academic performance.[128] Consistency of judgment is measured by the number of circular triads given by a respondent; a circular triad occurs, for example, when a subject prefers A to B, B to C, but C to A. The fewer the triads, the more consistent the subject. When two versions of this measure were used on two college samples, the results for both samples indicated that the relation between response consistency and grades is curvilinear. The best grades are made by those in the seventy-fifth to eightieth percentile of consistency. Grades for subjects who are almost perfectly consistent are about the same as those for subjects at the fiftieth percentile of consistency, and the overall linear correlation runs about .30 to .35. Furthermore, this measure is essentially independent of academic aptitude. The authors state that the inclusion of this measure in a predictor battery can raise multiple correlations by .10 to .15.

A study using this technique on law school samples reported no relationship between consistency and grades.[129] However, since the use of other measures on law students also results in negative findings, this group might be dissimilar in some unknown respects from the general population of undergraduate students.[130]

The findings on consistency and performance appear promising, although their meaning is not clear. A common-sense interpretation would be that students who are very consistent are perhaps somewhat inflexible and rigid, and thus are less able to deal effectively with ambiguities in intellectual matters. On the other hand, subjects who are quite inconsistent are perhaps not intellectually systematic enough to organize the material they must deal with as students.

In research conducted by Messick and Frederiksen, small but positive correlations were obtained between scores on report-writing tests (which might be a measure of one type of academic skill) and certain scales of the Personality Research Inventory.[131] One use of the report-writing tests was to measure the ability to make discriminations on reports. This ability was related to personality characteristics such as tolerance of ambiguity and preference for intellectual things ("liking to think"), although the correlations were small. Such cognitive characteristics appear to have relevance for the prediction of school grades.

In connection with these findings on "liking to think," Field found that high achievers in college see themselves as having an "inquiring intellect" to a greater degree than low achievers.[132]

Measures of Aggression. The research on report-writing tests and the Personality Research Inventory also indicated that aggressiveness was inversely related to report-writing performance.[133] A few other studies also present data on the relationship between aggression and academic performance. Bresee found that for high school students, the greater the hostility and extrapunitiveness, the lower the level of achievement,[134] but he did not adequately control for ability. Stoner found that the low achievers in a group of bright high school males were more defensive and resentful than the high achievers.[135] Shaw and Grubb observed that highly intelligent, low-achieving male high school students scored significantly higher than their achieving counterparts on three measures of hostility.[136] One other study on the college level reported findings consistent with those observed by Shaw and Grubb.[137]

The Hr Scale. Gough developed the Hr Scale for the prediction of academic performance.[138] The items were taken from other instruments such as the MMPI, and new items were also formulated. They seem to refer to a variety of personality characteristics rather than a single dimension. On three samples of high school seniors, the scale correlated with academic performance from .52 to .63. Correlations of intelligence and performance ran from .62 to .80. Multiple correlations using Hr and intelligence as predictors ranged from .72 to .85, which indicates that Hr makes an independent contribution to prediction. Gough states that on both high school and college levels, average correlations between the Hr Scale and academic performance run from .35 to .45; and in a battery with intelligence, the multiple correlation is estimated at .57.[139] The scale content suggests that traits such as seriousness of purpose and persistence are directly associated with academic performance. Among other studies using the Hr Scale, Bendig and Klugh found that the scale contributed independently to the multiple prediction of college grades.[140] Bendig used the Hr Scale with the Edwards Need Achievement Scale and a vocabulary scale to predict the academic performance of male college students.[141] He found that a battery composed of the vocabulary test and the need-achievement test was the best predictor. The addition of the Hr Scale did not significantly increase the multiple correlation, apparently because the Hr Scale was significantly correlated with the vocabulary test.

Measures of Defensiveness. Two investigations focus on a variable that might be termed "defensiveness about revealing perceived personal inadequacies." Hackett developed a scale consisting of all MMPI items which discriminated high- and low-achieving male college freshmen.[142] These items were found to be essentially unrelated to a measure of ability, and they significantly increased the level of prediction obtained through the use of the ability measure alone. These items suggest that one factor that is related to academic performance is defensiveness in revealing weakness.

Brown and Abeles developed a test of "facade orientation" by using a vocabulary test containing nonexistent words.[143] The measure of facade was the number of fake words checked as known. For samples of male and female college students this measure correlated negatively with grades. No sex differences were observed. However, the facade score was also correlated with scores on a vocabulary test (a measure of ability). Thus, the facade score might not have been related to grades if ability had been controlled.

Measures of Extrasensory Perception. Two studies deal with the relationship between academic performance and measures of extrasensory perception (ESP). One finds that the phenomena of precognition and clairvoyance do not enter into college students' objective test scores.[144] An investigation by Anderson on the secondary school level reports a positive relationship between level of ESP score and academic performance.[145] However, intelligence was not controlled, and since a number of studies report a positive association between ESP and intelligence, the positive findings of this study probably are spurious.

Summary of Findings: Single-Variable Studies

In considering a summary of the preceding research on personality factors, it should be borne in mind that in many respects the resulting portrait is overdrawn. While distillation and simplification are useful for summarizing purposes, some of the characterizations are supported only by flimsy evidence.

First, the student whose academic achievement is high tends to have better study habits and more favorable attitudes toward school than the student whose academic achievement is lower. He is also likely to have a greater interest in the course areas in which he is superior. His interests tend to have greater clarity and to have been chosen independently of the influence of others. He tends to exhibit a greater degree of achievement motivation, to be more independent, and to have more impulse control, since he is able to delay immediate gratifications in the interest of long-run goals to a greater extent than the student who performs at a lower level. Furthermore, the high-achieving student, is likely to have less anxiety in test-taking situations, so that his performance is less affected by this factor. Superficially at least, he appears to be more introverted than his low-achieving counterpart. When self-images are compared, the high achiever is more likely to have a positive self-image. Finally, the research suggests that the high achiever has greater cognitive flexibility, is less hostile, and is less defensive about revealing personal inadequacy than is the low achiever.

These conclusions need qualification in terms of their generality across educational levels and for the sexes. In general, far more research has been conducted at the college level than at other levels; therefore, the conclusions are more relevant for college students. In addition, the findings are more representative of males than females. However, insofar as it has been possible to assess sex differences, the literature presents no evidence of any major differences between males and females in the relationship between personality variables and academic performance—that is, in no case is a variable positively related for males and negatively related for females.

In conclusion, it is worth reiterating that this summary provides a much clearer picture than the literature warrants. Many of the relationships just described are tenuous at best, and it is undoubtedly true that the state of knowledge regarding the relation between personality variables and achievement is still so tentative that it cannot be used confidently for practical purposes, such as for college admissions.

II. MULTIVARIATE APPROACHES

Almost all the studies reviewed to this point focused upon the effects of a single variable or at most a few variables. However, some of the most recent research suggests a new trend toward a broad, multivariate approach. These studies direct attention to the measurement of a larger number of variables, to the assessment of their interrelations, and to the discovery of those dimensions of personality which are independently related to academic achievement.

The Findings

Illustrative of the trend toward multivariate analysis are four college-level studies using the Edwards Personal Preference Schedule. Most of these studies have been cited earlier in connection with single personality variables, but they have not been assessed in terms of the consistency with which they are related to performance across a number of personality variables. One study found no differences between different achievement groups within different ability levels.[146] The other three studies showed some positive findings. Thus, Krug reported that overachievers were higher on needs for achievement, order, and endurance, but were lower on need for affiliation and heterosexuality.[147] One investigation found that low-ability students whose school performance was adequate were higher on needs for deference, endurance, and dominance, but lower on autonomy, exhibitionism, and affiliation, as compared with low-ability students who were failing.[148] The third study found that overachieving male freshmen were higher than underachievers on the needs for achievement, order, intraception, and consistency, but were lower on needs for nurturance, affiliation, and change (variety).[149] Over- and underachievers were then distinguished according to ability level. That is, groups of low-ability overachievers and underachievers and high-ability overachievers and underachievers were defined. Low-ability overachievers were found to be higher on heterosexuality than the underachievers; and high-ability underachievers were higher on need for consistency than their overachieving counterparts. The findings from these three studies suggest a pattern. First, all three find that overachievers are lower on need for affiliation; second, two report that overachievers are higher on need for achievement, order, and endurance.

Holland, using the California Psychological Inventory and an aptitude test on a sample of high-ability male and female college freshmen, found that for males, the best predictor battery included the mathematics score from the aptitude test and personality scores on socialization, social presence, and femininity.[150] For females, the best battery included verbal aptitude and scores on social presence, responsibility, achievement via conformance, and femininity. The level of the multiple correlations is about the same for males and females. Holland also notes that there is considerable variability from one college to another in the level of the correlations between the personality test and academic performance.

Brown studied the characteristics of college girls nominated by faculty as outstanding students.[151] Girls who were nominated did not always have high grades, but 57 per cent had A averages. The teachers perceived these girls as being quite different from other girls who had high grades but were not nominated as outstanding students. Specifically, the nominated girls were characterized as intelligent, curious, independent, flexible, original, friendly, and analytic. The nominated and nonnominated girls were then compared on a variety of measures independent of faculty ratings. On the basis of these measures, the nominated girls were characterized by a high degree of social maturity, moderate impulse expression, and low repression. In addition, the nominated girls were low on conformity and on degree of integration with the student peer culture.

The well-known study by Stern, Stein, and Bloom used a large number of measures referring to cognitive, motivational, and behavioral dimensions.[152] In one part of the research, 63 highly intelligent students (above the ninetieth percentile on an intelligence test) were studied. Three variables showed appreciable correlations with academic performance: one was a spatial relations test that measured the ability to visualize a configuration when it was moved into different positions; the second was a measure of relevant thinking in the classroom; and the third was an instructor rating of the quality and extent of participation in the classroom.

In a succeeding phase of the study, an activities index was developed to measure the students' likes and dislikes for various activities. Application of this measure to high and low achievers showed that the former were more restrained in social and heterosexual activities, more interested in theoretical and abstract cognitive matters, concerned with activities that were community-centered rather than primarily egocentric, preferred achievement of a scholarly nature rather than "success," and desired to establish the dominant role in relations with others.

A third aspect of this study involved the formulation of concepts defining two contrasting types of personality: stereopathic and nonstereopathic. Stereopathic personalities were expected to find difficulty with tasks involving ambiguity, abstraction, spontaneity, and departure from convention. It was expected that this personality type would find greater difficulty in the humanities and social science areas (presumably because these areas are more ambiguous). In addition, it was expected that stereopaths would have difficulty in their social adjustment at the university because of its emphasis upon humanistic and liberal education. Furthermore, it was predicted that stereopaths would choose practical vocations such as medicine, law, business, and engineering. Stereopaths and nonstereopaths were matched on ability. The findings showed that stereopaths performed less well than the nonstereopaths in the social science and humanities areas; they made poorer adjustments to college; and they did tend to choose such vocations as accounting and law, while the nonstereopaths did not.

Another study, which used more than 20 measures of ability, interests, personality, and temperament, reported that for male college seniors majoring in the physical sciences, the battery that best predicted academic performance included measures of general intelligence, mechanical interest, morale, stability, and activity level.[153] The addition of personality factors more than doubled the efficiency of prediction using ability measures alone.

Still another study on the college level undertook a factor analysis of a number of motivational measures.[154] The data showed that academic performance was strongly related only to a verbal aptitude factor and had very low relationships with motivational factors—mainly a "freedom from a neurotic orientation to study tasks" factor.

Turning to research at the high school level, Nason attempted to delineate the factors related to the achievement of gifted high school students.[155] Among subjects matched on sex and intelligence but differing widely in level of achievement, the high achievers more often felt that their parents expected them to attend college (true for boys); they also had higher scores on measures of "sense of personal freedom" and "freedom from nervous symptoms." High-achieving girls were higher on social adjustment.

On the junior high school level, Bishton studied a sample of intellectually superior boys and girls.[156] From a number of measures of achievement, personality, and goals used for a factor analysis, 16 factors emerged. High academic performance was described as related to only one of these factors—a general achievement factor characterized by high ability, high socioeconomic status, male sex, and self-preoccupation.

A study of male and female seventh-graders at four schools was conducted by McGuire and associates.[157] Forty-one measures of ability, personality, and social behavior were used for purposes of multiple correlation analysis and factor analysis. Although there was variability by schools and by sex in the particular predictors which correlated best with grades, three measures had appreciable relations with academic performance across sex and schools: two were sociometric measures of peer acceptance and social effectiveness; the other was a measure of motivation and attitudes toward school. Multiple correlations of predictor variables with grades were about .80 at the four schools, and the correlations for males were about equal to those for females.

A study by d'Heurle, Mellinger, and Haggard attempted to assess the factors related to the level and patterns of achievement in a group of gifted third grade children (at or above the ninetieth percentile of ability).[158] Performance was measured by achievement tests. Students exhibiting a high level of general achievement were found to be sensitive to and accepting of adult standards, were better adjusted, had good work habits, were persistent, and were able to express hostility in culturally approved ways. High achievement in arithmetic tended to be related to the ability to get along with adults, to creativity, and to skill in symbol manipulation. High reading achievers were more withdrawn and insecure with adults. High spelling achievers were more passive, dependent on authority, and less creative. Thus, this study suggests that different types of personality factors may be related to performance in specific subject areas.

Summary of Findings: Multivariate Studies

In these multivariate studies so many different kinds of measures and concepts are used that it is difficult to summarize them. To obtain some sense of order from the findings, we have performed what might be called an "intuitive" factor analysis of them. This procedure has involved a number of steps. First, we have gone back over each of the studies and simply listed the major variables reported as being related to academic performance. This list is presented in Table 1. We have then examined this list, asking whether there are underlying dimensions in terms of which the variables might be categorized. On the basis of this examination, the list is classified according to six underlying dimensions. These, along with the names of the variables constituting each, are presented in Table 2.

TABLE 1.   LISTING OF PERSONALITY VARIABLES
ASSOCIATED WITH ACADEMIC PERFORMANCE
IN MULTIVARIATE STUDIES

Higher levels of performance tend to be associated with:
1. higher achievement motivation
2. higher need for order
3. more endurance
4. greater socialization
5. greater social presence
6. greater femininity
7. higher conformance
8. greater curiosity
9. greater independence
10. greater flexibility
11. greater originality
12. greater social maturity
13. moderate impulsivity (lack of constrictedness)
14. greater ability to visualize a configuration when moved
15. more relevant thinking in the classroom
16. more class participation (quality and frequency)
17. restraint in social behavior
18. greater liking for thinking
19. less stereopathy
20. higher morale
21. greater stability
22. higher activity level
23. greater freedom from neurotic orientation to study
24. lower need for affiliation
25. responsibility
26. low conformity to peer group standards

Dimension I consists of those variables indicative of what might be called "Social Maturity in the Student Role." It is composed of factors such as social presence or composure, responsibility, and socialization. The findings thus suggest that social maturity is positively related to academic achievement.

Dimension II identifies an "Emotional Stability" pattern defined by characteristics such as high morale and freedom from neurotic orientation to study. The findings suggest that high emotional stability is associated with a higher level of performance.

A third dimension is labeled the "Achievement Motivation Syndrome." Personality characteristics associated with this dimension are: high achievement motivation, high activity level, and high endurance or persistence. Such characteristics appear to be positively related to performance.

A fourth dimension groups together a set of variables referring to cognitive style. It suggests that intellectual curiosity is positively related to performance; the person who likes to think, whose classroom participation is both frequent and of high quality, and who is intellectually flexible rather than rigid is likely to exhibit a higher level of performance.

TABLE 2. CLASSIFICATION OF PERSONALITY VARIABLES ASSOCIATED WITH ACADEMIC PERFORMANCE IN MULTIVARIATE STUDIES

Item[a]

Dimension I:
Social Maturity in the Student Role

5. greater social presence
25. responsibility
12. greater social maturity
4. greater socialization
17. restraint in social behavior

Dimension II:
Emotional Stability

20. higher morale
21. greater stability
23. greater freedom from neurotic orientation to study

Dimension III:
Achievement Motivation Syndrome

1. higher achievement motivation
22. higher activity level
3. more endurance

Item

Dimension IV:
Cognitive Style

8. greater curiosity
10. greater flexibility
11. greater originality
14. greater ability to visualize a configuration when moved
15. more relevant thinking in class
16. more class participation (quality and frequency)
18. greater liking for thinking
19. less stereopathy

Dimension V:
Achievement via Conformance

2. higher need for order
6. greater femininity
7. higher conformance

Dimension VI:
Achievement via Independence

24. lower need for affiliation
9. greater independence
26. low conformity to peer group standards
13. moderate impulsivity (lack of constrictedness)

[a] Multivariate study items describe characteristics of the high achiever.

The fifth and sixth dimensions suggest the presence of two apparently opposite patterns, both of which are positively related to performance. The student characterized by the fifth dimension as having high need for orderliness and being high on femininity and conformance is likely to achieve at a higher level than the student who is low on these characteristics. On the face of it, the term "femininity" may be somewhat misleading since it applies to both male and female high achievers. As used here, this term implies not that the male who is high on this factor is effeminate, but that he is more docile, passive, and obedient in classroom behavior. In general, such characteristics are more often associated with the female role, and for this reason these types of behavior have sometimes been considered to be descriptive of femininity. For present purposes, however, it is more important to focus upon the particular behavioral characteristics rather than on the label which summarizes them.

The sixth dimension appears to be the opposite of the fifth. We have labeled it "Achievement via Independence." This pattern is defined by characteristics such as low need for affiliation, independence, low conformity to peer group standards, and moderate impulsivity (an individual who is neither highly compulsive nor highly hedonistic).

The presentation of the fifth and sixth dimensions as independent dimensions rather than opposite poles of the same dimension raises the question of how directly contrasting characteristics can lead to the same outcome—namely, a higher level of performance. We suggest that this can happen because each set of characteristics may occur within a unique social context. That is, expectations defining the student role may vary from one school to another or even from one department to another within a school, so that in some contexts independence is rewarded more highly than conformity, while in others the opposite is true. Thus, any set of personality characteristics may have relevance for academic achievement only when the variables describing the social environment are taken into consideration.

While this ad hoc analysis does provide some meaningful ordering of the findings, what is needed is a series of studies designed to assess whether such dimensions actually exist and whether they are independent. Such research should be carried out at different educational levels, for both males and females, and at different ability levels, because the nature of the dimensions might be different for each of these. The case of different ability levels is particularly relevant because some of the studies providing the basis for this summary have been carried out on samples that were highly selected with regard to ability—samples of either highly gifted or low-ability students. Consequently, we do not know whether the findings can be generalized to other ability levels.

FINAL SUMMARY AND CONCLUSIONS

The findings of both the single-variable and multivariate studies will be synthesized by using the ad hoc dimensions formulated to summarize the results of the multivariate studies and assessing the degree to which the findings of the single-variable studies seem to fit into this structure. The degree of alignment between the two is presented in Table 3. It can be seen that most of the findings summarized for the single-variable studies seem, intuitively, to fit rather well into the dimensions summarizing the multivariate investigations.

Thus, Table 3 suggests that the dimension "Social Maturity in the Student Role" parallels the single-variable findings which indicate that higher levels of performance tend to be associated with better study habits, more positive attitudes toward school, and less hostility. The dimension "Emotional Stability" coincides with the findings suggesting that test anxiety is positively related to scholastic standing. Dimension III, "Achievement Motivation Syndrome," aligns with the single-variable data that suggest a positive association between achievement motivation and school performance. The finding that higher-achieving students show greater flexibility in problem-solving seems to parallel the findings summarized under Dimension IV, "Cognitive Style." Several findings from the single-variable studies appear to fit rather well into the context of Dimension VI, "Achievement via Independence." They suggest that the student who exhibits a higher

TABLE 3.   ALIGNMENT OF FINDINGS FROM SINGLE-
VARIABLE STUDIES WITH DIMENSIONS SUM-
MARIZING MULTIVARIATE STUDIES

Multivariate Summary Dimensions	*Alignment of Single-Variable Findings*
	Higher levels of performance tend to be associated with:
I. Social Maturity in the Student Role	better study habits and more positive attitudes toward school less hostility
II. Emotional Stability	less test anxiety
III. Achievement Motivation Syndrome	higher achievement motivation
IV. Cognitive Style	greater flexibility in problem-solving
V. Achievement via Conformance	_____
VI. Achievement via Independence	more independence and/or introversion less impulsivity greater independence in choice of vocational interests

Non-aligned Findings:
more positive self-image
less defensiveness about revealing
personal inadequacy
greater interest in content areas
of high achievement

degree of independence and/or introversion, a lower degree of impulsivity, and a greater degree of independence in the choice of vocational interests is likely to show higher performance.

A few of the single-variable findings do not seem to fit readily into this structure. Those that do not align indicate that: the higher-achieving student tends to have a more positive self-image; he tends to be more interested in the course areas in which he achieves best; his vocational interests have greater clarity; and he is less defensive about revealing personal inadequacy.

The ordering of findings is presented mainly to structure what would otherwise be a mass of unrelated and perhaps chaotic observations. While this structure is largely arbitrary, it at least sensitizes us to some of the major constellations of variables whose relationships need to be assessed in future work.

The order with which we have infused the findings should not lead the reader to think that we can, at present, be very confident about the state of knowledge regarding the relationship between personality characteristics and academic performance. In most cases these relationships are quite weak, and, as we have seen, the findings are often inconsistent. Essentially, we think that the literature presents a somewhat disappointing picture. Yet we do not conclude that personality variables are simply not very useful as predictors. The current disappointing state of affairs may be more a reflection upon how personality variables have been used rather than upon their absolute usefulness. That is to say, up to now almost all the studies reviewed conceive of the individual as if he were operating in a social vacuum. It might be, however, that personality characteristics are useful in predicting academic performance only when the social setting in which that performance takes place is conceptualized and used as a significant variable. The characteristics of the social setting and the ways in which these interact with personality so as to affect the level of academic performance are topics discussed in the next two chapters.

NOTES TO CHAPTER 5

1. Burgess, Elva, "Personality Factors of Over- and Under-Achievers in Engineering," *Journal of Educational Psychology*, vol. 47, 1956, pp. 89–99; Maher, Howard, "Follow-up on the Validity of a Forced-Choice Study Activity Questionnaire in Another Setting," *Journal of Applied Psychology*, vol. 43, 1959, pp. 293–295; Schutter, Genevieve, and Howard Maher, "Predicting Grade-Point Average with a Forced-Choice Study Activity Questionnaire," *Journal of Applied Psychology*, vol. 40, 1956, pp. 253–257.

2. Bonner, Leon, "Factors Associated with the Academic Achievement of Freshmen Students at a Southern Agricultural College," *Dissertation Abstracts*, vol. 17, 1957, pp. 266–267; Christensen, Clifford M., "A Note on Borow's College Inventory of Academic Adjustment," *Journal of Educational Research*, vol. 50, 1956, pp. 55–58; Diener, Charles L., "A Comparison of Over-achieving and Under-achieving Students at the University of Arkansas," *Dissertation Abstracts*, vol. 17, 1957, p. 1692; Knaak, Nancy, "A Study of the Characteristics of Academically Successful and

Unsuccessful Freshmen Women Who Entered Northwestern University in the Fall of 1954," *Dissertation Abstracts,* vol. 17, 1957, pp. 304–305.

3. Jex, Frank B., and Reed M. Merrill, "Intellectual and Personality Characteristics of University of Utah Students," *Journal of Educational Research,* vol. 53, 1959, pp. 118–120.

4. Carter, Harold D., "Improving the Prediction of School Achievement by the Use of the California Study Methods Survey," *Educational Administration and Supervision,* vol. 45, 1959, pp. 255–260.

5. Kerns, Byron L., "A Study of Under-achieving and Over-achieving First Semester College Freshmen as Revealed by the Way in Which They View the College Situation and Themselves as College Students," *Dissertation Abstracts,* vol. 17, 1957, p. 2500.

6. Birney, Robert C., and Marc J. Taylor, "Scholastic Behavior and Orientation to College," *Journal of Educational Psychology,* vol. 50, 1959, pp. 266–274.

7. McGauvran, Mary E., "A Study of the Relationship Between Attitude Toward School and Scholastic Success at the High School and College Level," *Dissertation Abstracts,* vol. 15, 1955, pp. 2482–2483.

8. Brown, William F., and Wayne H. Holtzman, "A Study-attitudes Questionnaire for Predicting Academic Success," *Journal of Educational Psychology,* vol. 46, 1955, pp. 75–84; Holtzman, Wayne H., W. F. Brown, and W. W. Farquhar, "The Survey of Study Habits and Attitudes: A New Instrument for the Prediction of Academic Success," *Educational and Psychological Measurement,* vol. 14, 1954, pp. 726–732.

9. Sie, Georgiana D. W., "The Relationship of Two Experimental Measures of Student Motivations to Academic Success in College," *Dissertation Abstracts,* vol. 15, 1955, pp. 1556–1557.

10. Lum, Mabel K. M., "A Comparison of Under- and Overachieving Female College Students," *Journal of Educational Psychology,* vol. 51, 1960, pp. 109–114.

11. Ahmann, J. Stanley, William L. Smith, and Marvin D. Glock, "Predicting Academic Success in College by Means of a Study Habits and Attitude Inventory," *Educational and Psychological Measurement,* vol. 18, 1958, pp. 853–857.

12. Anderson, Robert P., and James E. Kuntz, "The 'Survey of Study Habits and Attitudes' in a College Counseling Center," *Personnel and Guidance Journal,* vol. 37, 1959, pp. 365–368.

13. Chahbazi, Parviz, "Analysis of Cornell Orientation Inventory Items on Study Habits and Their Relative Value in Prediction of College Achievement," *Journal of Experimental Education,* vol. 27, 1958, pp. 135–142.

14. O'Leary, M. J., "The Measurement and Evaluation of the Work Habits of Overachievers and Underachievers to Determine the Relationship of These Habits to Achievement," *Dissertation Abstracts,* vol. 15, 1955, pp. 2104–2105.

15. Norton, Daniel P., "The Relationship of Study Habits and Other Measures to Achievement in Ninth Grade General Science," *Journal of Experimental Education,* vol. 27, 1959, pp. 211–217.

16. Cronbach, Lee J., *Essentials of Psychological Testing.* Harper and Brothers, New York, 1949.

17. Travers, Robert M. W., "Significant Research on the Prediction of Academic Success," in Donahue, W. T., and associates, editors, *The Measurement of Student Adjustment and Achievement,* University of Michigan Press, Ann Arbor, 1949.

18. Collins, Charles C., "The Relationship of Breadth of Academic Interest to Academic Achievement and Academic Aptitude," *Dissertation Abstracts,* vol. 15, 1955, pp. 1782–1783.

19. Hewer, Vivian H., "Vocational Interest-Achievement-Ability Interrelationships at the College Level," *Journal of Counseling Psychology,* vol. 4, 1957, pp. 234–238; Melton, Richard S., "Differentiation of Successful and Unsuccessful Premedical Students," *Journal of Applied Psychology,* vol. 39, 1955, pp. 397–400.

20. Burgess, Elva, *op. cit.*

21. Shepler, Warren Davis, "A Study of Scholastic Achievement in Secondary School Science in Relation to Pupils' Relative Preference for this Subject," *Dissertation Abstracts,* vol. 16, 1956, pp. 1376–1377.

22. Kerns, Byron L., *op. cit.*

23. Knaak, Nancy, *op. cit.*

24. Diener, Charles L., *op. cit.*

25. Phelps, Morris O., "An Analysis of Certain Factors Associated with Under-Achievement Among High School Students," *Dissertation Abstracts,* vol. 17, 1957, pp. 306–307.

26. Rust, Ralph, and F. J. Ryan, "The Strong Vocational Interest Blank and College Achievement," *Journal of Applied Psychology,* vol. 38, 1954, pp. 341–345.

27. Cronbach, Lee J., *op. cit.*

28. Bloomberg, M., "The Prediction of Scholastic Success Through the Use of a Forced-Choice Problems-and-Attitude Inventory," *Dissertation Abstracts,* vol. 15, 1955, p. 2566; Knaak, Nancy, *op. cit.;* McQuary, John P., "Some Differences Between Under- and Overachievers in College," *Educational Administration and Supervision,* vol. 40, 1954, pp. 117–120; Sherwood, Emily J., "An Investigation of the Relationship Between the Academic Achievement and Goal Orientations of College Students," *Dissertation Abstracts,* vol. 17, 1957, p. 2924; Weitz, Henry, and Robert M. Colver, "The Relationship Between the Educational Goals and the Academic Performance of Women: A Confirmation," *Educational and Psychological Measurement,* vol. 19, 1959, pp. 373–380; Weitz, Henry, Mary Clark, and Ora Jones, "The Relationship Between Choice of a Major Field and Performance," *Educational and Psychological Measurement,* vol. 15, 1955, pp. 28–38.

29. Knaak, Nancy, *op. cit.;* McQuary, John P., *op. cit.*

30. Weitz, Henry, and Robert M. Colver, *op. cit.;* Weitz, Henry, Mary Clark, and Ora Jones, *op. cit.*

31. Weigand, George, "Goal Aspiration and Academic Success," *Personnel and Guidance Journal,* vol. 31, 1953, pp. 458–461.

32. Cooper, Matthew N., "To Determine the Nature and Significance, If Any, of Certain Differences in the Social and Personal Adjustment of Fifty-One Successful and Fifty-One Non-Successful Students at Texas Southern University," *Dissertation Abstracts,* vol. 16, 1956, p. 497.

33. Armstrong, Marion E., "A Comparison of the Interests and Social Adjustment of Under-Achievers and Normal Achievers at the Secondary School Level," *Dissertation Abstracts,* vol. 15, 1955, p. 1349.

34. Edwards, T. Bentley, and Alan B. Wilson, "The Specialization of Interests and Academic Achievement," *Harvard Educational Review,* vol. 28, 1958, pp. 183–196.

35. McClelland, David C., and associates, *The Achievement Motive.* Appleton-Century-Crofts, Inc., New York, 1953.

36. *Ibid.,* p. 237.

37. Weiss, Peter, Michael Wertheimer, and Byron Groesbeck, "Achievement Motivation, Academic Aptitude, and College Grades," *Educational and Psychological Measurement,* vol. 19, 1959, pp. 663–666.

38. Burgess, Elva, *op. cit.*

39. Chahbazi, Parviz, "Use of Projective Tests in Predicting College Achievement," *Educational and Psychological Measurement,* vol. 16, 1956, pp. 538–542.

40. Walter, Verne Arthur, "The Effect of Need for Academic Achievement on the Performance of College Students in Learning Certain Study Skills," *Dissertation Abstracts,* vol. 17, 1957, p. 1384.

41. Haber, Ralph N., "The Prediction of Achievement Behavior by an Interaction of Achievement Motivation and Achievement Stress," *Dissertation Abstracts,* vol. 17, 1957, pp. 2686–2687.

42. Krumboltz, John D., and William W. Farquhar, "Reliability and Validity of the N-achievement Test," *Journal of Consulting Psychology,* vol. 21, 1957, pp. 226–228.

43. Parrish, John, and Dorothy Rethlingshafer, "A Study of the Need to Achieve in College Achievers and Non-Achievers," *Journal of General Psychology,* vol. 50, 1954, pp. 209–226.

44. Mitchell, James V., Jr., "An Analysis of the Factorial Dimensions of the Achievement Motivation Construct," *Journal of Educational Psychology,* vol. 52, 1961, pp. 179–187.

45. Rosen, Bernard C., "The Achievement Syndrome: A Psychocultural Dimension of Social Stratification," *American Sociological Review,* vol. 21, 1956, pp. 203–211.

46. Hills, John R., "Needs for Achievement, Aspirations, and College Criteria," *Journal of Educational Psychology,* vol. 49, 1958, pp. 156–161.

47. Bendig, Albert W., "Comparison of the Validity of Two Temperament Scales in Predicting College Achievement," *Journal of Educational Research*, vol. 51, 1958, pp. 605–609; Krug, Robert E., "Over- and Underachievement and the Edwards Personal Preference Schedule," *Journal of Applied Psychology*, vol. 43, pp. 133–136; Weiss, Peter, Michael Wertheimer, and Byron Groesbeck, *op. cit.*

48. Christensen, Clifford M., *op. cit.;* Cooper, Matthew N., *op. cit.;* Worell, Leonard, "Level of Aspiration and Academic Success," *Journal of Educational Psychology*, vol. 50, 1959, pp. 47–54.

49. Christensen, Clifford M., *op. cit.*

50. Bresee, Clyde W., "Affective Factors Associated with Academic Underachievement in High-School Students," *Dissertation Abstracts*, vol. 17, 1957, pp. 90–91.

51. Hills, John R., *op. cit.*

52. Weiss, Peter, Michael Wertheimer, and Byron Groesbeck, *op. cit.*

53. Melikian, Levon H., "The Relationship Between Edwards' and McClelland's Measures of Achievement Motivation," *Journal of Consulting Psychology*, vol. 22, 1958, pp. 296–298.

54. Hills, John R., *op. cit.*

55. Mitchell, James V., Jr., *op. cit.*

56. In addition to the studies which have observed low reliability cited earlier, a review by Krumboltz also concludes that projective measures of achievement motivation have low reliability. See Krumboltz, John D., "Measuring Achievement Motivation: A Review," *Journal of Counseling Psychology*, 1957, vol. 4, pp. 191–198.

57. Mitchell, James V., Jr., *op. cit.*

58. For work illustrative of this problem, see Atkinson, John W., "Motivational Determinants of Risk-Taking Behavior," *Psychological Review*, vol. 64, 1957, pp. 359–372; Clark, Russell A., Richard Teevan, and Henry N. Ricciuti, "Hope of Success and Fear of Failure as Aspects of Need for Achievement," *Journal of Abnormal and Social Psychology*, vol. 53, 1956, pp. 182–186; Martire, John G., "Relationships Between the Self-Concept and Differences in the Strength and Generality of Achievement Motivation," *Journal of Personality*, vol. 24, 1956, pp. 364–375; McDavid, John, "Some Relationships Between Social Reinforcement and Scholastic Achievement," *Journal of Consulting Psychology*, vol. 23, 1959, pp. 151–154; Mitchell, James V., Jr., "Goal-Setting Behavior as a Function of Self-Acceptance, Over- and Underachievement, and Related Personality Variables," *Journal of Educational Psychology*, vol. 50, 1959, pp. 93–104.

59. French, John W., *The Description of Personality Measures in Terms of Rotated Factors*. Educational Testing Service, Princeton, N.J., 1953, p. 257.

60. Weigand, George, *op. cit.*

61. Burgess, Elva, *op. cit.*

62. Gilmore, John V., "A New Venture in the Testing of Motivation," *College Board Review*, vol. 15, 1951, pp. 221–226.

63. Carrier, Neil A., "Stress, Personality, and Performance on Course Examinations," *Dissertation Abstracts*, vol. 17, 1957, p. 1400.

64. Merrill, Reed M., and Daniel T. Murphy, "Personality Factors and Academic Achievement in College," *Journal of Counseling Psychology*, vol. 6, 1959, pp. 207–210.

65. Erb, Everett D., "Conformity and Achievement in College," *Personnel and Guidance Journal*, vol. 39, 1961, pp. 361–366.

66. Douvan, Elizabeth, and Joseph Adelson, "The Psychodynamics of Social Mobility in Adolescent Boys," *Journal of Abnormal and Social Psychology*, vol. 56, 1958, pp. 31–44.

67. McClelland, David C., and associates, *op. cit.*

68. Young, Lloyd R., "Parent-Child Relationships Which Affect Achievement Motivation of College Freshmen," *Dissertation Abstracts*, vol. 17, 1957, p. 3111.

69. Parsons, Talcott, *The Social System*. The Free Press, Glencoe, Ill., 1951.

70. Merrill, Reed M., and Daniel T. Murphy, *op. cit.*

71. Krug, Robert E., *op. cit.*

72. Weigand, George, "Adaptiveness and the Role of Parents in Academic Success," *Personnel and Guidance Journal*, vol. 35, 1957, pp. 518–522.

73. Frederiksen, Norman O., and S. Donald Melville, "Differential Predictability in the Use of Test Scores," *Educational and Psychological Measurement*, vol. 14, 1954, pp. 647–656; Frederiksen, Norman O., and Arthur C. F. Gilbert, "Replication of a Study of Differential Predictability," *Educational and Psychological Measurement*, vol. 20, 1960, pp. 759–767.

74. MacArthur, Russell S., "An Experimental Investigation of Persistence in Secondary School Boys," *Canadian Journal of Psychology*, vol. 9, 1955, pp. 42–54.

75. McDavid, John, "Some Relationships Between Social Reinforcement and Scholastic Achievement," *Journal of Consulting Psychology*, vol. 23, 1959, pp. 151–154; Schroder, Harold M., and David E. Hunt, "Failure Avoidance in Situational Interpretation and Problem Solving," *Psychological Monographs*, vol. 71, 1957.

76. Douvan, Elizabeth, and Joseph Adelson, *op. cit.*

77. Bendig, Albert W., "The Validity of Two Temperament Scales in Predicting Student Achievement in Introductory Psychology," *Journal of Educational Research*, vol. 50, 1957, pp. 571–580; Bendig, Albert W., "Comparative Validity of Empirical Temperament Test Keys in Predicting Student Achievement in Psychology," *Journal of Educational Research*, vol. 51, 1958, pp. 341–348; Gilmore, John V., *op. cit.;* Grooms, Robert R., and Norman S. Endler, "The Effect of Anxiety on Academic Achievement," *Journal of Educational Psychology*, vol. 51, 1960, pp. 299–304; Klugh, Henry E., and Albert W. Bendig, "The Manifest Anxiety

and ACE Scales and College Achievement," *Journal of Consulting Psychology,* vol. 19, 1955, p. 487; Mitchell, James V., Jr., "Goal-Setting Behavior as a Function of Self-Acceptance . . . ," *op. cit.;* Spielberger, Charles D., and William G. Katzenmeyer, "Manifest Anxiety, Intelligence, and College Grades," *Journal of Consulting Psychology,* vol. 23, 1959, p. 278.

78. Grooms, Robert R., and Norman S. Endler, *op. cit.;* Klugh, Henry E., and Albert W. Bendig, *op. cit.;* Spielberger, Charles D., and William G. Katzenmeyer, *op. cit.*

79. Klugh, Henry E., and Albert W. Bendig, *op. cit.*

80. Grooms, Robert R., and Norman S. Endler, *op. cit.*

81. Bendig, Albert W., "The Validity of Two Temperament Scales . . .," *op. cit.;* Bendig, Albert W., "Comparative Validity of Empirical Temperament Test Keys . . .," *op. cit.*

82. Mitchell, James V., Jr., "Goal-setting Behavior as a Function of Self-Acceptance . . .," *op. cit.;* Gilmore, John V., *op. cit.*

83. Reese, Hayne, "Manifest Anxiety and Achievement Test Performance," *Journal of Educational Psychology,* vol. 3, 1961, pp. 132–135.

84. Morgan, Elmer, Brian Sutton-Smith, and B. G. Rosenberg, "Age Changes in the Relation Between Anxiety and Achievement," *Child Development,* vol. 31, 1960, pp. 515–519.

85. Carrier, Neil A., *op. cit.*

86. Smith, William F., and F. C. Rockett, "Test Performance as a Function of Anxiety, Instructor, and Instructions," *Journal of Educational Research,* vol. 52, 1958, pp. 138–141.

87. Sarason, Irwin G., "Test Anxiety and the Intellectual Performance of College Students," *Journal of Educational Psychology,* vol. 52, 1961, pp. 201–206.

88. Phillips, Beeman N., Edwin Hindsman, and Carson McGuire, "Factors Associated with Anxiety and Their Relation to the School Achievement of Adolescents," *Psychological Reports,* vol. 7, 1960, pp. 365–372.

89. Sarnoff, Irving, and associates, "Test Anxiety and the 'Eleven-plus' Examinations," *British Journal of Educational Psychology,* vol. 29, 1959, pp. 9–16.

90. Sarason, Irwin G., "Intellectual and Personality Correlates of Test Anxiety," *Journal of Abnormal and Social Psychology,* vol. 59, 1959, pp. 272–275.

91. Alpert, Richard, and Ralph N. Haber, "Anxiety in Academic Achievement Situations," *Journal of Abnormal and Social Psychology,* vol. 61, 1960, pp. 207–215.

92. Phillips, Beeman N., Edwin Hindsman, and Carson McGuire, *op. cit.*

93. Travers, Robert M. W., *op. cit.*

94. Bloomberg, M., *op. cit.*

95. Kerns, Byron L., *op. cit.*

96. Birney, Robert C., and Marc J. Taylor, *op. cit.*

97. Krug, Robert E., *op. cit.*

98. Gebhart, G. Gary, and Donald P. Hoyt, "Personality Needs of Under- and Over-Achieving Freshmen," *Journal of Applied Psychology,* vol. 42, 1958, pp. 125–128.

99. Merrill, Reed M., and Daniel T. Murphy, *op. cit.*

100. Beach, Leslie R., "Sociability and Academic Achievement in Various Types of Learning Situations," *Journal of Educational Psychology,* vol. 51, 1960, pp. 208–212.

101. Knaak, Nancy, *op. cit.*

102. Phelps, Morris O., *op. cit.*

103. Cooley, Charles H., *Social Organization,* Charles Scribner, New York, 1912; Mead, George H., *Mind, Self, and Society,* University of Chicago Press, Chicago, 1934; Cottrell, Leonard S., Jr., "The Analysis of Situational Fields in Social Psychology," *American Sociological Review,* vol. 7, 1942, pp. 370–382; Sullivan, Harry S., *The Interpersonal Theory of Psychiatry,* W. W. Norton and Co., Inc., New York, 1953.

104. Brim, Orville G., Jr., "College Grades and Self-Estimates of Intelligence," *Journal of Educational Psychology,* vol. 45, 1954, pp. 477–484.

105. Lum, Mabel K. M., *op. cit.*

106. Stevens, Peter H., "An Investigation of the Relationship Between Certain Aspects of Self-Concept Behavior and Students' Academic Achievement," *Dissertation Abstracts,* vol. 16, 1956, pp. 2531–2532.

107. Shaw, Merville C., Kenneth Edson, and Hugh M. Bell, "The Self-Concept of Bright Underachieving High School Students as Revealed by an Adjective Check List," *Personnel and Guidance Journal,* vol. 39, 1960, pp. 193–196.

108. McDavid, John, *op. cit.*

109. Reeder, T. A., "A Study of Some Relationships Between Level of Self-Concept, Academic Achievement, and Classroom Adjustment," *Dissertation Abstracts,* vol. 15, 1955, p. 2472.

110. Schroder, Harold M., and David E. Hunt, *op. cit.*

111. Bendig, Albert W., and Martin R. Gluck, "Concomitants of Achievement Test Frustration in College Students," *Journal of Educational Research,* vol. 49, 1956, pp. 365–371.

112. Martire, John G., *op. cit.*

113. Schulman, Jacob, "A Comparison Between 9th and 12th Grade Students on Self-Estimates of Abilities and Objective Scores on the Differential Aptitude Tests," *Dissertation Abstracts,* vol. 16, 1956, pp. 285–286.

114. Hackett, Herbert R., "The Use of M.M.P.I. Items to Predict

College Achievement," *Personnel and Guidance Journal,* vol. 39, 1960, pp. 215–217.

115. Jensen, Vern H., "Influence of Personality Traits on Academic Success," *Personnel and Guidance Journal,* vol. 36, 1958, pp. 497–500.

116. Burgess, Elva, *op. cit.*

117. Frick, J. W., "Improving the Prediction of Academic Achievement by Use of the MMPI," *Journal of Applied Psychology,* vol. 39, 1955, pp. 49–52; Frick, J. W., and Helen E. Kenner, "A Validation Study of the Prediction of College Achievement," *Journal of Applied Psychology,* vol. 40, 1956, pp. 251–252.

118. Quinn, Stanley B., "Relationship of Certain Personality Characteristics to College Achievement," *Dissertation Abstracts,* vol. 17, 1957, p. 809.

119. Gallese, Arthur J., Jr., "Personality Characteristics and Academic Achievement in School of Engineering Students," *Dissertation Abstracts,* vol. 19, 1959, pp. 3022–3023.

120. Clark, John H., "Grade Achievement of Female College Students in Relation to Non-Intellective Factors: MMPI Items," *Journal of Social Psychology,* vol. 37, 1953, pp. 275–281; Stone, David R., and G. R. Ganung, "A Study of Scholastic Achievement Related to Personality as Measured by the Minnesota Multiphasic Inventory," *Journal of Educational Research,* vol. 50, 1956, pp. 155–156.

121. Hoyt, Donald P., and Warren T. Norman, "Adjustment and Academic Predictability," *Journal of Counseling Psychology,* vol. 1, 1954, pp. 96–99.

122. Drake, Lewis E., and Eugene R. Oetting, "An MMPI Pattern and a Suppressor Variable Predictive of Academic Achievement," *Journal of Counseling Psychology,* vol. 4, 1957, pp. 245–247.

123. Travers, Robert M. W., *op. cit.*

124. Burgess, Elva, *op. cit.;* Clark, Selby G., "The Rorschach and Academic Achievement," *Personnel and Guidance Journal,* vol. 36, 1958, pp. 339–341; Cooper, James G., "The Inspection Rorschach in the Prediction of Academic Success," *Journal of Educational Research,* vol. 49, 1955, pp. 275–283; Rust, Ralph, and F. J. Ryan, "Relationship of Some Rorschach Variables to Academic Behavior," *Journal of Personality,* vol. 21, 1953, pp. 441–456; Sopchak, Andrew L., "Prediction of College Performance by Commonly Used Tests," *Journal of Clinical Psychology,* vol. 14, 1958, pp. 194–197.

125. Horrall, Bernice M., "Academic Performance and Personality Adjustment of Highly Intelligent College Students," *Genetic Psychology Monographs,* vol. 55, 1957, pp. 3–83.

126. Schmeidler, Gertrude R., Marjory J. Nelson, and Marjorie Bristol, "Freshman Rorschachs and College Performance," *Genetic Psychology Monographs,* vol. 59, 1959, pp. 3–43.

127. McArthur, Charles C., and Stanley King, "Rorschach Configura-

tion Associated with College Achievement," *Journal of Educational Psychology,* vol. 45, 1954, pp. 492–498.

128. Gulliksen, Harold, David R. Saunders, and Ledyard R. Tucker, *Ability to Make Consistent Judgements in Paired Comparisons as a Predictor of Academic Achievement,* Preliminary Report, Educational Testing Service, Princeton, N.J., 1954.

129. Hills, John R., and Walter J. Raine, "Pair-Comparisons Consistency and Grades in Law School," *Journal of Applied Psychology,* vol. 44, 1960, pp. 94–96.

130. See Hills, John R., *op. cit.*

131. Messick, Samuel, and Norman Frederiksen, *Response Set as a Measure of Personality.* Educational Testing Service, Princeton, N.J., 1958.

132. Field, Lewis W., "Personality Correlates of College Achievement and Major Areas of Study," *Dissertation Abstracts,* vol. 14, 1954, pp. 1344–1345.

133. Messick, Samuel, and Norman Frederiksen, *op. cit.*

134. Bresee, Clyde W., *op. cit.*

135. Stoner, William G., "Factors Related to the Underachievement of High School Students," *Dissertation Abstracts,* vol. 17, 1957, pp. 96–97.

136. Shaw, Merville C., and James Grubb, "Hostility and Able High School Underachievers," *Journal of Counseling Psychology,* vol. 5, 1958, pp. 263–266.

137. Shaw, Merville C., and Donald J. Brown, "Scholastic Underachievement of Bright College Students," *Personnel and Guidance Journal,* vol. 36, 1957, pp. 195–199. It might be noted that even though these last three studies control for ability, they do not define over- and underachievement according to the criterion discussed in Chapter 2— that is, they use the discrepancy between observed ability and observed grades rather than the difference between predicted grades and obtained grades. For this reason, the groups are more accurately called high and low achievers.

138. Gough, Harrison, "The Construction of a Personality Scale to Predict Scholastic Achievement," *Journal of Applied Psychology,* vol. 37, 1953, pp. 361–366; Gough, Harrison, "What Determines the Academic Achievement of High School Students?" *Journal of Educational Research,* vol. 46, 1953, pp. 321–331.

139. Gough, Harrison, "The Construction of a Personality Scale . . .," *op. cit.*

140. Bendig, Albert W., and Henry E. Klugh, "A Validation of Gough's Hr Scale in Predicting Academic Achievement," *Educational and Psychological Measurement,* vol. 16, 1956, pp. 516–523.

141. Bendig, Albert W., "Comparison of the Validity of Two Temperament Scales . . .," *op. cit.*

142. Hackett, Herbert R., *op. cit.*

143. Brown, William F., and Norman Abeles, "Facade Orientation and Academic Achievement," *Personnel and Guidance Journal,* vol. 39, 1960, pp. 283–286.

144. Heinlein, Julia, and Christian P. Heinlein, "What Is the Role of ESP in Objective College Testing at the College Level?" *Journal of Psychology,* vol. 46, 1958, pp. 319–328.

145. Anderson, Margaret, "The Relationship Between Level of ESP Scoring and Student Class Grade," *Journal of Parapsychology,* vol. 23, 1959, pp. 1–18.

146. Demos, George D., and Ludwig J. Spolyar, "Academic Achievement of College Freshmen in Relation to the Edwards Personal Preference Schedule," *Educational and Psychological Measurement,* vol. 21, 1961, pp. 473–479.

147. Krug, Robert E., *op. cit.*

148. Merrill, Reed M., and Daniel T. Murphy, *op. cit.*

149. Gebhart, G. Gary, and Donald P. Hoyt, *op. cit.*

150. Holland, John L., "The Prediction of College Grades from the California Psychological Inventory and the Scholastic Aptitude Test," *Journal of Educational Psychology,* vol. 50, 1959, pp. 135–142.

151. Brown, Donald R., "Non-Intellective Qualities and the Perception of the Ideal Student by College Faculty," *Journal of Educational Sociology,* vol. 33, 1960, pp. 269–278.

152. Stern, George C., Morris I. Stein, and Benjamin S. Bloom, *Methods in Personality Assessment.* The Free Press, Glencoe, Ill., 1956.

153. Stone, Solomon, "The Contribution of Intelligence, Interests, Temperament, and Certain Personality Variables to Academic Achievement in a Physical Science and Mathematics Curriculum," *Dissertation Abstracts,* vol. 18, 1958, pp. 669–670.

154. Michael, William B., Robert A. Jones, and W. A. Trembly, "The Factored Dimensions of a Measure of Motivation for College Students," *Educational and Psychological Measurement,* vol. 19, 1959, pp. 667–671.

155. Nason, Leslie J., *Academic Achievement of Gifted High School Students.* University of Southern California Press, Los Angeles, 1958, p. 92.

156. Bishton, Rodger, "A Study of Some Factors Related to Achievement of Intellectually Superior Eighth-Grade Children," *Journal of Educational Research,* vol. 51, 1958, pp. 203–208.

157. McGuire, Carson, and associates, "Dimensions of Talented Behavior," *Educational and Psychological Measurement,* vol. 21, 1961, pp. 3–38.

158. d'Heurle, Adna, Jeanne C. Mellinger, and Ernest A. Haggard, "Personality, Intellectual, and Achievement Patterns in Gifted Children," *Psychological Monographs,* vol. 73, 1959.

Chapter 6

Sociological Determinants

THE STUDIES DISCUSSED IN CHAPTER 5 viewed the individual as an isolated unit. They were not concerned with the social environments in which individuals function. The question they chose to emphasize was: Does personality have any general effects on academic achievement?

The sociological studies to be reviewed in this chapter take two forms, both of which differ from the psychological studies. One type examines the effects of role relationships on academic achievement. An example would be a study of the student-teacher relationship in which the degree of congruence between student and teacher definitions of the student's role is measured. The association between congruence and level of academic performance would then be assessed. One might find that the more closely a student's definition of his role agrees with the teacher's definition, the more likely the student is to exhibit a high level of performance. This approach is distinguished from the personality studies because it asks whether characteristics of social settings have any general effects on performance irrespective of the personality of the individual.

A second type of sociological study assesses the effects of various ecological and demographic characteristics upon academic performance. These investigations examine variables such as socioeconomic status, sex of the student, religion, rural-urban background, and the like. As we shall see, these variables are related to performance because they symbolize certain uniformities of personality. That is, positions in the social structure such as socioeconomic status and sex tend to produce certain similarities in personality among the occupants of these positions. Some of these personality characteristics are, in turn, related to academic achievement. Studies of this type are thus related to the studies reviewed in the preceding chapter. What is distinctively sociological about them, however, is that they show that personality characteristics pertinent to achievement are not simply randomly distributed in the population; rather, they tend to be systematically associated with positions in the social structure.

This chapter reviews and evaluates findings from both of these approaches. It begins with a review of the demographic and ecological findings; next it discusses the effects of specific role relationships; and finally it summarizes findings from both types of studies.

I. EFFECTS OF DEMOGRAPHIC AND ECOLOGICAL VARIABLES

Socioeconomic Status as a Determinant of Academic Performance

Of all the ecological and demographic factors to be discussed, the major variable in terms of the sheer quantity of research is socioeconomic status (SES). Most of the studies to be reviewed measure SES by some objective technique rather than by subjective ratings. The objective techniques all involve the combining or weighting of scores on variables such as occupation, education, income, attendance at private or public school, area of residence, and the like so as to produce an index of the position of the student's family in the status hierarchy.

We wish first to consider how such a measure of SES can be predictive of school performance. The answer is that SES is a *derivative* or summarizing variable. Persons of different socioeconomic status face different kinds of life situations, and in adapting to them, they may develop different sets of values and life styles.[1] In short, SES symbolizes a variety of values, attitudes, and motivations related to academic performance. There are two major factors symbolized by SES: one is intelligence; the other is what may be referred to as the "achievement syndrome."

SES and Intelligence. One factor positively associated with SES is intelligence. This finding is well documented,[2] but it raises a question concerning the degree to which SES and intelligence are independently related to academic performance. One study found that when SES is controlled, the correlation between intelligence and grades is not lowered.[3] On the other hand, when intelligence was controlled, correlations between SES and grades were lowered from a range of .37 to .47 to a range of .20 to .32. In another study, a traditional intelligence test and a "culture free" test were used to predict achievement test scores.[4] When SES was controlled, none of the correlations between intelligence and the criterion decreased very much. When intelligence was controlled, the original correlations between SES and the criterion were reduced from about .30 to .20.

If, as we have said, SES is a summarizing variable, it is to be expected that when any of the variables it summarizes (such as IQ) are controlled, relationships between SES and performance should be decreased. Since the relationship of SES to achievement was not totally erased when IQ was controlled, SES appears to summarize more than intelligence. In other words, if students are equated for intelligence, variations in social class are still associated with variations in achievement. Therefore, SES must also summarize other variables.

SES and the Achievement Syndrome. Another variable associated with SES is achievement motivation—or more appropriately perhaps, an achievement syndrome. Rosen found that achievement motivation is directly related to SES.[5] Students who exhibit high levels of motivation tend to come from higher status levels. Both achievement motivation and SES were directly related to the grades of high school students. However, when motivation was controlled, the relation between SES and grades was almost erased. This illustrates what was stated before; namely, that SES summarizes other variables.

Another aspect of the achievement syndrome is what may be

called achievement values. They include, among others, these beliefs: (1) that it is possible to manipulate the environment; (2) that there is value in delaying immediate pleasure for the sake of long-run gratifications; and (3) that there is value in shedding affective ties to the family of orientation if these will interfere with mobility.[6] Students who adhere to these values tend to exhibit higher levels of career aspiration.

Evidence indicates that this set of beliefs is related to SES and is also associated with educational aspiration.[7] As with achievement motivation, when achievement values are controlled, the relation between SES and educational aspiration disappears. Strodtbeck found that achievement values were related to over- and under-achievement, and that they were independent of achievement motivation.[8] His findings suggest, therefore, that the use of achievement values and achievement motivation together may increase the efficiency of predicting academic performance. Schneider and Lysgaard showed that belief in the value of delayed gratification varies directly with SES.[9] Brim and Forer also demonstrated that the belief in the value of planning for the future is directly associated with SES.[10] Other studies find a direct association between SES and level of educational and occupational aspiration.[11] With the exception of the work by Rosen and by Strodtbeck, these investigations are not concerned with the prediction of academic performance. However, the achievement syndrome seems to be directly relevant to this question.

Research Findings. Of the research reviewed here, 13 studies report that SES is directly related to academic performance.[12] That is, the higher one's social status, the higher his level of performance. This relationship holds for all educational levels.

Of special interest are six studies whose findings contrast with these results.[13] They find that SES is inversely related to performance.

The apparent contradiction in these studies needs to be resolved. It is important to note at the outset that the samples used in the studies that find SES to be directly related to performance are different in certain respects from the samples used in those that observe an inverse relationship. Of the latter, five of the six studies show inverse relationships when the college performance of public school graduates is compared with that of private school graduates. Furthermore, in four of these investigations, the subjects were males who attended some of the very top eastern Ivy League colleges,[14] where the preparatory school graduates (largely from the most prestigious eastern preparatory schools) were likely to come mainly from upper-class backgrounds, while the public school graduates were likely to be largely of middle- and upper-middle-class origins.

Since most of the research on SES and academic performance does not sample the upper-class segment of the SES range, we suggest that the inconsistency between the results of the various studies referred to at the outset can be accounted for by differences in the SES range sampled. The situation is probably as follows: The relationship between SES and academic performance is positive through most of the SES range, but at the upper SES levels, it is inverse. When the SES sample does not include this upper segment, positive relations will be found. When the sample does include the upper range and does not go below the middle class, inverse relations will be found.

The preceding explanation is, of course, a statistical one. There remains the question of the meaning of the discrepancy on a theoretical level. We turn now to this question.

Two studies of the performance of Princeton students found that public school graduates are superior academically to private school graduates during the freshman year and that this superiority is maintained during the sophomore year, even though the two groups do not differ with regard to ability.[15] It seems reasonable to assume, as have the authors in this research, that private school students tend to be of higher SES than public school students. Another writer, in discussing findings of this sort, also suggests that private school graduates represent mainly the upper classes.[16] In the Princeton studies the authors present a possible explanation for the findings. First, since the public school graduates are from somewhat lower SES, college is an important means of enhancing status; private school graduates, on the other hand, need only to maintain their status level. For the latter group, therefore, simply graduating from college may be more important than the academic record they establish. Thus, differential motivation may be operative.

A second interpretation would be that because private schools have a more directed regimen, their graduates encounter difficulty in adapting to the less structured college environment. If true, differences in college performance would be due to structural differences between private schools and public schools. At the present time, this remains an open question awaiting the results of additional research.

The first interpretation has received attention from McArthur,[17] who asserts that the eastern upper classes hold values that are not consistent with the American success orientation. Whereas this orientation stresses the future as the important time, the individual as the important person, and doing (achieving) as the important aspect of the person, among the upper-class group the important time is the past, the important persons are lineal ancestors, and "being" (a gentleman) is the most important aspect of the person. The latter is a portrayal of an aristocratic ideal in which behavior is oriented toward propriety in contrast to achievement. Presumably, the upper and middle classes differ in terms of these values.

These status groups also differ in terms of methods of child training. The parents of the middle-class public school group gear early training toward achievement and mobility; the parents of the upper-class private school group orient early training toward proper, gentlemanly behavior. These training and value differences may be reflected in the school achievement of the children. This probably constitutes the underlying theoretical meaning expressed in the earlier statistical explanation. In short, the inconsistency in the two sets of studies relating socioeconomic status to academic performance is more apparent than real. It can be resolved on both a statistical and a theoretical level.

Summary and Evaluation. The research shows that socioeconomic status is usually positively related to academic performance, but that on the college level the relationship is inverse when the range of SES runs from the upper to the middle class. The apparent inconsistency is interpretable in terms of personality and value differences between social status categories.

SES is a significant variable in the study of performance because it summarizes systematic variations in attitudes, motivations, and value systems that are related to such performance. While two underlying factors have been pointed out (intelligence and the achievement syndrome), this is probably not an exhaustive list. What is needed is a thorough review of the differences in personality, value systems, and behavior that are related to SES. Such class-related variables can then be applied to the study of achievement in school.

Another neglected area of research concerns the question of sex differences in the relation of SES to academic performance. It might be that SES is directly related to performance for males, but not for females. In addition, the class-related personality characteristics that are predictive of academic performance might be qualitatively different for males and females. These possibilities have not yet been researched.

Social class differences may also partly determine the quality of student-teacher interaction. For example, one might ask how the interaction of middle-class teachers with lower-class students affects characteristics of the student-teacher relationship. Davidson and Lang found that children's perceptions of their teacher's favorability or unfavorability toward them were directly related to social class.[18] This suggests that SES-related behavioral characteristics may affect the treatment students receive from teachers.

In short, SES may summarize a number of other factors in addition to the ones noted earlier. Further research is needed.

Sex Differences in Academic Performance

Throughout this review, sex has been used as one major point of reference for describing the research findings. However, most studies are not concerned with the study of sex differences. We now examine those studies that are concerned with this question.

The Findings. The studies that assess the relation between sex and academic performance show that females have higher academic performance than males.[19] The evidence in Chapter 4 also clearly suggests that the correlation between intelligence and performance is higher for females than for males; that is, the performance of females is more nearly in accord with their measured ability than is the case for males.

In addition, a few more specialized findings are of interest. In a longitudinal study on the elementary school level, Hughes found that when ability was controlled, the reading achievement of girls was superior to boys through the fourth grade; however, beyond this grade the sex differences were not significant and did not consistently favor the girls.[20]

In a most interesting study, Shaw and McCuen attempted to determine whether there is any specific academic level at which underachievement begins.[21] They used students in the top 25 per cent of the school population with regard to ability and classified them as achievers or underachievers on the basis of their cumulative grade-point averages in grades 9, 10, and 11. A student whose IQ was higher than 110 and whose grade-point average was below the mean for his class was classified as an underachiever;[22] one whose grade-point average was above his class mean and whose IQ was above 110 was classified as an achiever. By eliminating some students, the authors ensured that the comparison groups had equal means and variances in their intelligence scores. They also controlled for sex. After the groups were selected, the academic record of each student for grades 1 through 11 was obtained and the performance of each group at each grade level was computed. When the higher- and lower-achieving males were compared, the data showed a significant difference between the two groups beginning at the third grade and increasing at each grade level up to grade 10, where it began to decrease, though it remained statistically significant.

Comparison of higher- and lower-achieving females presents quite a different picture. Through grade 5 those females who are later to become low achievers tend to exceed the higher achievers in grade-point average. At grade 6 the higher achievers attain a higher grade-point average for the first time, and this difference increases every year until grade 10. It is interesting to note that the start of the drop for the lower-achieving group roughly coincides with the onset of puberty. In contrast, the low-achieving males show a predisposition toward lower performance very early in their elementary school careers.

Summary and Evaluation. The findings on sex differences indicate that the level of academic performance of females is higher than that of males. Second, they suggest that the development of underachievement may follow a different pattern for females than for males. In all likelihood the significance of these findings can be understood in terms of a variety of differences in attitudes and behavior which result from the fact that males and females are socialized differently. Each sex must learn to play a different role, and the attitudes and values associated with sex-role learning may help to explain sex differences in academic performance.

In the first place, academic success probably has different significance for males than for females. Within the context of the cultural definition of the male role, academic success is an instrumental goal having important implications for later career success. For females the instrumental aspect of academic performance may not be as important, since integration with the occupational system is less crucial for the female role. Because academic success for males is considered more significant in terms of later occupational success, family pressures on them to do well in school are probably stronger than they are for females. If academic success is more directly involved with the male's affective ties to his family, the school might be more likely to become an arena in which either compulsive conformity to, or rebelliousness from, parental expectations may occur. Compulsive conformity would lead to overachievement, and rebelliousness, to underachievement.

Another consideration is that female teachers far outnumber male teachers, especially in the elementary and high schools. This being the case, we might speculate that teacher definitions of the student role include more characteristics of the female sex role. That is, the model of a good student is a female model. If this is true, then for the male, deviation from the student role actually constitutes a confirmation of his masculinity. This point has been made by Parsons in an attempt to account for certain patterns of aggressive behavior.[23]

If these interpretations have any validity, they may help to explain why the phenomena of over- and underachievement are more often observed for males than for females.[24] While it is interesting to speculate about these sex differences, more research is required both to document this evidence further and to specify the sources of the differences. Particularly interesting are the questions raised by the longitudinal studies—such as why the development of underachievement for girls follows a different pattern than that for boys.

Miscellaneous Ecological and Demographic Characteristics

The scattering of research on the relationship between academic performance and other ecological and demographic factors includes studies on religion, school size, age, geographic region, and academic load.

Religious Background. Some evidence suggests that with regard to religion, Jewish students outperform non-Jewish students. Strodtbeck found this to be true when he compared Jewish high school students with their Italian Catholic counterparts.[25] However, many of the differences between these two groups seemed attributable to the effects of socioeconomic status rather than religion. That is, while Jews were more likely to have characteristics related to high academic achievement, when SES was controlled, the effects of religion disappeared. One other study found that Jews were more likely to be high achievers than students of other religions.[26]

Because some evidence suggests the presence of differences in the value systems of different religious groups further study is warranted. The work to date indicates, for example, that relative to the Italian Catholic value system, the Jewish culture places greater emphasis on the value of education and confers more prestige upon the scholar. Presumably this emphasis upon scholarship fits into a value system which places great importance upon rationality, future time orientation, and the like. Whether such achievement-related values are unique to particular religious groups or are associated more generally with differences in socioeconomic status should be ascertained through further investigation.

Regional and Rural-Urban Variation. A few studies have looked at the effects of regional and community differences upon academic performance. In a summary of some of these findings, Rossi states that students in the South score lower on achievement tests than do students in the North.[27] He points out, however, that these studies do not hold intelligence constant. Therefore, the poorer achievement of southern students could be due to lower ability, to inferior schools, or perhaps to both.

Studies of rural-urban background find that students from urban areas have higher levels of academic performance than students from less populated areas.[28] However, the study by Washburne finds that the relation of urbanism to academic performance does not hold for the students who come from major metropolitan areas (500,000 or more), perhaps because of the greater heterogeneity of students from such areas. Another study found that while urban students were higher on aptitude than rural students, they were no different in academic performance.[29] However, the rural students tended to be registered in schools of agriculture, and urban students in business or arts and sciences colleges; consequently, it is difficult to interpret the results of these studies because the grades are not comparable.

While these findings indicate that northern students outperform southern students and that urban students outperform their rural counterparts, the meaning of such findings is ambiguous. A number of factors, either singly or in combination, could account for these results. Thus, urban students may obtain higher scores on intelligence tests. Moreover, they may come from higher SES levels and the urban schools may be educationally superior to rural schools. At present, the research findings do not allow us to assess these possibilities.

Age. Three studies of the effects of age on academic performance in the elementary school reach contradictory conclusions. One of these finds that under-age children have lower school achievement than children of normal age for the grade and equivalent ability.[30] Another finds that under-age children are somewhat superior in achievement,[31] and a third shows little effect of age.[32]

While no generalization can be made on the basis of these studies, on other educational levels—for example, on the high school level—one might expect that students who are older than the average would exhibit lower levels of academic performance, since academic difficulty may have slowed their progress. This could be the case even if ability were controlled.

High School Size. Two studies examine the relationship between size of high school and academic performance in college. One of these finds that graduates of smaller high schools tend to receive lower grades, even though they are not lower on intelligence.[33] The other study finds size to be unrelated to college performance.[34]

While these studies permit no generalization, it is suggested that if school size were found to have a consistent relation with college performance, this would probably be a result of differences in facilities, teacher salaries, and the like. Should this factor be systematically assessed, we would expect a curvilinear relationship between size and performance. Small high schools are probably found more frequently in rural areas, and their facilities and teacher salaries are likely to be inferior. At the other extreme, very large high schools are most likely to be found in congested urban areas where the schools suffer from overcrowding, inadequate facilities, and the presence of large proportions of economically and socially underprivileged youth. Medium-sized schools would be representative of communities able to provide facilities at a pace more or less in keeping with population increases.

Academic Load. Five studies find that academic load (number of courses carried) has little or no effect upon school performance.[35] For low-ability students, however, academic load is inversely related to grades. Because there is so little variability in load at any educational level, this probably cannot be considered to be an important factor.

II. EFFECTS OF SPECIFIC ROLE RELATIONSHIPS

This section is concerned with whether there are characteristics of a student's social relationships that affect his academic performance. To answer this question, research is presented on various characteristics of the student-to-student, student-to-teacher, and student-to-family relationships.

The Student-to-Student Relationship

In studies of the student-to-student relationship the social acceptability of the student is the dimension that has received most attention. Many studies map the sociometric structure of the student peer group by assessing the network of friendship choices and by computing the number of choices that are received and reciprocated. The relationship between popularity and academic performance is then observed. In addition to the popularity dimension, other topics dealt with have been, for example, the effects of the value systems of peer group cliques upon individual performance.

The Findings. On the college level, Johnson studied the relationship of actual scholastic performance to peer ratings of popularity and peer ratings of performance.[36] He found that ratings of performance were directly related to both ratings of popularity and actual performance, and that ratings of popularity were also directly related to actual performance. He did not control for sex or intelligence. If intelligence had been controlled, the relationship between popularity and performance might have disappeared.

Zumwinkle investigated factors associated with the compatibility of 85 pairs of female college roommates.[37] He hypothesized that compatible roommates are homogeneous with regard to a variety of characteristics—among them, grades. He found however, that compatibility was not associated with homogeneity in grades. Although our concern is with the determinants of grades, not compatibility, this study at least points to another variable (roommate interaction) that may be pertinent to the prediction of academic performance. Future research might consider the effects on grades of various characteristics of roommate interaction.

On the high school level, several studies have dealt with the relation of acceptability and popularity to academic performance. Edminston and Rhoades found that the best battery for the prediction of performance included a sociometric measure of social acceptance.[38] Ryan and Davie observed small positive relationships between social acceptability and grades.[39] However, this relationship was not consistent at different high schools, and popularity tended to be related to quantitative aptitude. The authors did not assess the relationship between popularity and grades with aptitude held constant. A third study used separate groups of males and females matched on intelligence but differing in school grades.[40] The different achievement groups within each sex were then compared on various trait ratings obtained from their classmates of the same sex. For boys, the data suggested that those with average grades were more likely to obtain trait ratings indicative of social acceptability—that is, students with average grades were better accepted than students with very high or very low grades. For girls, social acceptability trait ratings were directly related to grades: girls with higher grades had greater acceptability than girls with lower grades. However, girls with high grades were rated by their same-sex peers as being less acceptable to boys than girls with lower grades.

Coleman has shown how different aspects of the social structure of high schools can affect academic performance.[41] He found that among the criteria for membership in the "leading crowd" at different high schools in the Midwest, high scholarship ranks low compared to athletic ability. The members of the social elites in these high schools found it more undesirable to be seen as an intellectual than did nonmembers. And it was even less desirable for a girl to be perceived as an outstanding scholar than for a boy. Furthermore, at high schools where the peer culture placed a relatively low value on academic scholarship, the highest achieving students did not usually have the highest ability; but where the peer culture valued scholarly attainment more highly, the best students were more likely also to be the most intelligent. In short, the high-status cliques at many schools have explicit norms that tend to inhibit high levels of academic achievement. These are similar to norms among factory workers that have been found to restrict output.[42]

Coleman points out that the peer group rewards most highly excellence in areas in which a *group* represents the institution, such as athletics. Scholastic achievement, on the other hand, occurs on an individual basis. Coleman suggests that to raise the level of academic achievement, scholarly activity should be restructured so that outstanding individual achievement benefits the school as a whole. This could be done through interscholastic competition in debating, science projects, and the like. In short, he argues that the individualistic structure of competition for academic success needs to be shifted to a group basis so that the competitive context becomes intermural rather than intramural.

On the elementary school level, two studies find a positive relation between social acceptability and academic performance.[43] In both cases the relationship disappeared when intelligence was controlled.

Another elementary school investigation studied the relationship between students' liking or disliking for the classroom group and their own attitudes toward academic achievement.[44] The results showed that the attitudes toward academic performance of students who liked their group were similar to those they perceived the group as holding. The attitudes toward achievement of students who did not like their group were not related to those they perceived the group as holding. Although this study did not attempt to relate these findings to actual performance, it does illustrate the influence that perceived peer group standards can have upon individual students. Insofar as attitudes toward achievement are related to actual achievement, such findings become significant.

Summary and Evaluation. These studies show considerable variability in the relationships between sociometric measures of popularity and academic performance. The findings for the elementary school level suggest that the relationship between popularity and performance is positive, but the significance of the finding is open to question, since the relationship disappears when intelligence is controlled. This suggests that social acceptability may be a result rather than a determinant of academic performance. The rationale for this statement is that elementary school students may not be sufficiently autonomous to develop peer group norms independent of their teacher's attitudes. That is, peer norms regarding school achievement may be, in large part, reflections of teacher expectations. Thus, students who best meet these expectations (through high academic performance) may be the most popular among their peers. They may also be more likely to be the ones with the most ability.

On the high school level, the situation becomes more complicated because the findings are more variable. In one study popularity was independently related to performance, and in another it was not. A third suggested that the relationship between social acceptability and performance was positive for girls but curvilinear for boys. Perhaps the situation can be clarified by Coleman's findings which showed that the content of peer group norms influenced student attitudes toward academic achievement. For this reason the differences in findings might be attributed to variability in student value systems regarding achievement at various high schools. For example, a curvilinear relationship between popularity and performance for male students would suggest the presence of peer group norms that define the "gentleman's C" as the most desirable type of performance. A positive and direct relationship between popularity and performance might suggest the presence of peer group norms that value scholarly attainment.

At present one can do no more than speculate as to the reasons for differences in the findings. Further research along the lines illustrated by Coleman in which the attempt is made to understand status in the peer group in terms of the particular value systems defining peer group norms would be desirable. Most of the current research dealing with the social acceptability dimension pays insufficient attention to the content of the norms to which conformity is demanded.

The assessment of the normative structure of student subcultures should be accompanied by research on some related questions. For example, students are often members of several peer subgroups, and the possible effects of multiple group membership upon academic performance levels is one such question. Suppose, for example, that these different membership groups accord different priorities to scholarly attainment. What are the effects of such conflict on the individual student? Research on such questions promises to increase our understanding of the student-to-student relationship as a factor affecting academic performance.

The Student-Teacher Relationship

Chapter 2 pointed out that one reason for the less-than-perfect correlations between ability and academic performance was what might be called teacher "error." It noted that a grade is actually an index summarizing certain characteristics of the student-teacher relationship. One indication of this lies in the fact that ability usually is more highly correlated with scores on achievement tests than with teacher grades.

Studies dealing with the effects of the student-teacher relationship upon academic performance can be divided into two classes. First are those that focus on the degree of consensus between students and teachers with regard to expectations defining their respective roles. The degree of consensus then is used as a variable for predicting school grades. Second are studies dealing with the relation between specific kinds of teacher behavior and specific types of student behavior that presumably constitute responses to the acts of the teacher.

Congruence of Student and Teacher Role Expectations. At the college level, Yourglich asked students and teachers to list spontaneously the characteristics of the ideal student and ideal teacher.[45] The data show that students and teachers are more likely to agree on the definition of the student role than on that of the teacher role. Furthermore, agreement about the student role tends to increase from the freshman to the senior year, but no such trend is evident with regard to the teacher role. Characteristics frequently mentioned as part of the ideal student role were "diligence," "maturity," "cooperative," "intelligent," "dependable," and "integrity." Characteristics frequently mentioned as part of the ideal teacher role were "understanding," "ability to communicate," "integrity," "maturity," and "stimulating." This study did not use the congruence between student and teacher role definitions to predict student grades. However, such measures of consensus could be used for this purpose.

Kelley attempted to assess the factors responsible for discrepancies in achievement as measured by instructor grades and common departmental term-end examination grades.[46] The students who received higher instructor grades than examination grades differed from the students in the reverse situation. The former tended to be more conforming, compulsive, and insecure. They were also lower in ability. This finding suggests that behavioral characteristics of students interact with teacher expectations so as to produce grades from teachers that are not closely related to achievement as measured by objective examinations.

On the high school level, Battle explored the effects on school grades of the degree of congruency in student-teacher value patterns.[47] He hypothesized that students whose value patterns were closer to the teacher's ideal would have higher grades than students whose patterns diverged more from the teacher's ideal. With age, sex, and aptitude controlled, the findings lent support to the hypothesis. What is perhaps even more interesting is the implicit suggestion that some of the value dimensions need not be related to the instrumental aspects of the school situation in order to be predictive of school performance. Although one would normally expect that it is the task-relevant values such as diligence, integrity, and the like that are the important criteria used by the teacher in defining proper behavior for the student role and to which the successful student must conform, several of the value dimensions used in this study do not appear to have direct instrumental significance (among these are economic, political, and religious values). Thus, agreement with teacher values per se may be related to student achievement. In short, it may be that if the student shares the values of the teacher, he is more likely to do well in school even though such values are more or less irrelevant to explicitly defined criteria for the scholarship aspects of the student role. This is not to deny that the scholarship aspects are important; it is simply to point out that other considerations may also be involved.

A study by Carter also suggests that more than the scholarship aspects of the student role is involved in teacher grades.[48] He found that the sex of the student and the sex of the teacher interact to influence the degree of relationship between high school algebra grades and achievement test scores in algebra. Thus, when the teacher is a male, the correlation between algebra grades and scores on algebra achievement tests is higher for male students than for female students. When the teacher is a woman, there are no differences between male and female students in this correlation. However, for male teachers the *absolute* level of the correlations is higher for both male and female students. This indicates that the sex of the student has more influence on male instructors, but that beyond this, male teachers show greater objectivity in grading (assuming as we are that the achievement test score provides the truer measure of the student's learning). Female instructors are less objective, but the sex of the student is apparently not a factor influencing objectivity.

Two other studies deal with comparisons of perceptions of appropriate student conduct in high school situations by teachers, students, and parents. The first study showed that differences in perception between students on different grade levels were larger than differences among students, teachers, and parents.[49] The second study attempted to assess the relationships between students', teachers', and parents' definitions of the appropriate behavior for students in various situations.[50] Correlations on the order of .88 to .92 were observed among the perceptions of these three groups. Furthermore, there were certain sex differences in the perceptions: girls appeared to be more concerned with dimensions of student behavior involving etiquette, reputation, and appearance, and boys were more concerned with behavior involving the communication of ideas and efficiency. In short, the different perceptions of boys and girls seemed to be related to the performance of masculine and feminine roles. Neither study deals explicitly with the problem of predicting academic performance. Potentially, however, they could be applied to this question.

Getzels and Jackson, in their research on creativity, found that when students high in creativity but not correspondingly high in intelligence were compared with students high in intelligence but not correspondingly high in creativity, no differences in academic achievement appeared.[51] However, teachers preferred the latter group of students, perhaps because highly creative students are more difficult to deal with in class situations, since they are likely to think in terms that depart from a structured class agenda. This finding appears to contradict the findings of previously cited studies which suggest that teacher favorableness toward a student will result in higher grades, other things being equal. Perhaps these results can be reconciled by the interpretation that schools vary in breadth of definition of the student role. In some, the definition may be highly circumscribed, and in others, it may permit a wider range of behaviors, even though teachers may find certain kinds of class behavior preferable. In the latter type of school, there may be little relationship between student-teacher role congruence and academic performance. The Getzels and Jackson study might be illustrative of this.

On the elementary school level, Malpass administered a series of tests to eighth graders that were designed to measure student perceptions in five school areas: teachers, classmates, discipline, achievement, and school in general.[52] Responses were rated on a five-point scale of favorableness to each area. With ability controlled, correlations between these measures and two criteria of academic performance (grades and achievement test scores) were computed. It was found that favorable perceptions in the school areas were more highly related to grades than to achievement tests. In particular, favorable perceptions regarding teachers and achievement were most highly related to grades, the correlations ranging from .48 to .57. It is interesting that whereas most research finds that predictors correlate more highly with achievement test criteria than with grades, the findings of this study are the opposite. This suggests that favorable attitudes toward teachers and toward achievement result in better relations between student and teacher. The better relations may, in turn, lead to higher grades even though they may not objectively result in more learning, as measured by achievement tests.

Davidson and Lang studied children's perceptions of their teachers' feelings toward them in relation to their self-perceptions and their school achievement.[53] The measure of perception was a checklist of trait names. It was found that children's self-perceptions are similar to their perceptions of how their teacher feels toward them. Furthermore, favorableness of perceived feelings of the teacher was positively related to the teacher's actual rating of the child's school achievement. This relationship held true even when the social class background of the child was controlled. However, perceived favorability was directly related to social class, even when achievement rating was controlled. Thus, it appears that both social class and perceived favorableness are independently related to academic performance. A sex difference also appeared: girls perceived teachers as being more favorable than did boys. Furthermore, there was a slight tendency for girls to be rated higher in academic performance.[54] This suggests that the behavior of girls is more in line with teachers' definitions of the student role than is the behavior of boys. Perhaps this explains why a few studies have found that overachieving males tend to be higher on "femininity" scales.

A study by Baker and Doyle indicates that increasing teachers' knowledge of their elementary school pupils affects their grading behavior.[55] Teachers were provided with data on student achievement test scores, sociograms, student autobiographies, and anecdotal records. Thereafter, the correlation between ability and pupil grades decreased, suggesting that as teachers are provided with more information on students, their criteria for grading change. Perhaps increasing the teacher's awareness of individual differences leads him to adopt more flexible definitions of acceptable behavior within the student role.

Effects of Teacher Behavior on Student Behavior. The major research in this area has been conducted by Ryans.[56] The primary emphasis was on the assessment of dimensions describing teacher behavior, but the characteristics of pupil behavior that are related to teacher behavior were also considered. These studies were carried out on both the elementary and high school levels. On the elementary level, Ryans finds that certain characteristics of teacher behavior are associated with particular characteristics of pupil behavior. Originality and adaptability are defined as one dimension of teacher behavior. Associated with this is pupil behavior characterized by responsibility and high levels of class participation. A second dimension of teacher behavior is defined as responsible, well-planned, and systematic classroom procedure. Associated with this are pupil behaviors labeled as constructive, responsible, cooperative, and controlled.

On the high school level, it is interesting to note that characteristics of teacher behavior appear to be unrelated to the classroom behavior of the students. Perhaps at the high school level students are more deeply involved in the peer group and with the norms that it defines, and these norms may determine classroom behavior to a greater extent than do teacher expectations for the students.

In these studies Ryans did not attempt to relate student-teacher interaction patterns to the more traditional measures of academic performance. However, his research could readily be extended to deal with this problem. Studies could be conducted to assess the effects of interaction patterns upon achievement levels.

Rosenfeld and Zander have shown that teacher behavior may affect student aspiration level.[57] Using a high school sample, they found that the type of influence attempt used by teachers in interaction with students affects the degree to which aspirations of the student are congruent with his perceived capacity. Congruence occurs when teacher influence attempts are perceived as rewarding and legitimate, and lack of congruence occurs when influence is viewed as coercive and indiscriminate.

On the elementary school level, Christensen found that vocabulary and arithmetic achievement among fifth-graders was significantly greater for students of teachers who were high on a "warmth" scale.[58] Stringer has shown that differences in academic progress are due in part to teacher behavior.[59]

Summary and Evaluation. This body of research suggests a number of generalizations. First, the degree of congruence in student-teacher values, attitudes, and expectations is directly related to the academic performance of the student. Furthermore, this generalization holds even when the student-teacher similarity involves what seem to be task-irrelevant criteria. The findings also indicate the presence of sex differences in the definition of the student role.

Studies investigating the relationship between teacher behavior and student behavior have indicated an association between the two, although they suggest that student behavior is more independent of the acts of the teacher on the high school level than on the elementary level. While a few of these studies also find that teacher behavior affects the level of student academic performance, most have focused only upon interaction patterns, ignoring the relation of the patterns to performance.

A number of issues pertaining to this body of research need to be discussed. The findings showing that congruence in student-teacher values, attitudes, and role expectations is related to academic performance raise the question of the causal direction of such relationships. The degree of congruency could be either a determinant or a result of the level of academic performance—or there might be a feedback relationship between the two. With feedback, a moderate degree of congruency might result in a fairly high level of performance as indexed by the teacher's grades, and this, in turn, might serve to increase the student's identification with the teacher's values and attitudes, thus leading to an even higher subsequent level of academic performance. This question requires further work addressed to the assessment of time sequence in the operation of these variables. Furthermore, if student-teacher congruence is a causal factor determining grades, differential student awareness of teacher definitions of the student role may be a result of differences in social sensitivity. If so, the research in social perception would become relevant to the study of academic performance.

Another issue arising from this research concerns the suggestion of a relation between congruence and performance regardless of the content of the values and expectations used for computing congruence. However, what cannot be ascertained from the research is the degree of correlation between task-relevant and task-irrelevant congruence. It may be that when congruence occurs on task-relevant values, it also occurs on irrelevant values as a result of student identification with the teacher (a "halo" effect). But in the hypothetical case where congruence occurs only on task-irrelevant values, there may be no relation to academic performance. Further work is needed to assess this possibility.

Several other questions are raised but not answered by the research. For example, we know little about the conditions under which students' definitions of their roles converge or diverge from teacher definitions. What are the implications of a divergence between parental and teacher definitions of the student role for the manner in which the student defines his role? The question of the relative importance of the student's different reference groups in determining his value patterns is central here. The problem of the effects on academic performance of a situation where each reference group (that is, the peer group, teachers, the family) holds a different attitude toward school behavior is an especially interesting one; it is amenable to research of the type conducted by Newcomb in the Bennington study.[60] These kinds of questions deserve further investigation.

Family Relationships

Research on the relationship between family factors and academic performance falls into two categories. First, there are studies that focus on certain demographic characteristics of the family. Illustrative is research investigating the number of siblings and birth order in relation to school performance.

Second are studies concerned with the relation of various characteristics of family interaction to a student's school performance. In these studies, family interaction is not usually observed firsthand. Rather, inferences about the quality of interaction are made on the basis of information concerning attitudes of family members.

Sibling Structure of the Family. Bernstein states that family size is inversely related to academic performance; that is, the larger the number of siblings, the lower the level of school achievement.[61] Two facts may help to explain this relationship: first, Nisbet has pointed out that family size is inversely related to intelligence;[62] second, family size is inversely related to socio-economic status. Presumably, then, large families are significant for educational performance because they are likely to be of lower SES and lower intelligence as compared with smaller families. Of course, this fits in with findings cited earlier showing that students of lower SES exhibit lower achievement and lower intelligence than students of higher SES. However, Hunt cites evidence showing that the correlation between family size and intelligence holds within all occupational levels except at the very top (where it is possible to afford outside help in the care of children).[63] Thus, Hunt's discussion suggests that family size is independently (of SES) related to both intelligence and academic performance. In this connection, Bernstein and Nisbet suggest an alternative explanation; namely, that the association between family size and intelligence is due to the negative effects of large families on verbal development.[64]

Weitz and Wilkinson found that the academic performance of only children was significantly lower than that of a control group matched for scholastic aptitude.[65] This finding seems to conflict with Nisbet's report of an inverse correlation between family size and aptitude.[66] While the discrepancy cannot be resolved on the basis of evidence, it may be that only-child status is in some way qualitatively different from any situation in which there are two or more siblings. For example, the fact that the only child does not have the experience of a social relationship with sibs may interfere with the acquisition of social skills. This, in turn, might cause difficulties in social adjustment to school, and these might be reflected in lower academic performance. In short, it may be that the negative relationship between family size and achievement holds only for families of two or more children and that only-child status is a unique situation.

In a somewhat different kind of study, Schoonover assessed the effects on academic performance of birth order, sex of sibling, and age interval of siblings.[67] The only factor found to be related to performance was sex of sibling. Sibs of both sexes who had brothers exhibited higher performance on an achievement test than sibs who had sisters.

Brim found that cross-sex siblings have more traits of the opposite sex than do same-sex siblings.[68] This finding was even more pronounced for the younger cross-sex sibling. For example, a younger male sib with an older sister exhibits more feminine traits than a younger male sib with an older brother. Although this study was not concerned with the prediction of academic performance, the findings would seem to bear directly on this question. Thus, some studies have found that overachieving males tend to be higher on so-called femininity scales than underachieving males. Within this context, Brim's findings could be used to derive the prediction that male sibs with older sisters will exhibit higher academic achievement than male sibs with older brothers. It should be noted, however, that this hypothesis seems to conflict with the findings of Schoonover. Only additional research can clarify this issue.

Family Interaction Patterns. Strodtbeck has conducted research on the characteristics of family interaction, and one of his purposes was to relate these to the academic achievement of high school boys.[69] He found that characteristics of interaction such as the power distribution in the family and the degree of decision-making consensus were associated with certain personality characteristics which, in turn, were predictive of academic performance. In particular, the degree of decision-making consensus was related to the son's level of achievement motivation. Furthermore, the greater the degree of power the mother and the son have relative to the father, the higher will be the son's score on a test of achievement values. This latter finding is interpreted as an indication that the more power one has, the more likely he is to believe that the world can be rationally mastered, and the belief in one's ability to have some mastery over the world is presumably a prerequisite for believing in the value of achievement. While this study did not attempt to relate directly characteristics of family interaction to level of academic performance, the fact that such interaction characteristics are associated with achievement-related personality traits suggests that the interaction patterns themselves might be directly predictive of academic achievement.

Several other studies deal with the relationship between characteristics of family behavior and academic performance, although unlike the Strodtbeck research, they do not directly observe family interaction. Thus, one study of college males found that higher achievers had happier, more secure relations with the father.[70] This study did not control for ability, however.

In a study dealing with preparatory school boys of high intelligence who differed widely in academic performance, Kimball discovered that boys whose performance was quite low, unlike the higher achievers, had poor relations with their fathers; that is, the relationship had little warmth and the son feared the father.[71] In another study on the high school level, Tibbetts compared boys varying widely in academic performance level but matched for aptitude.[72] He found that the higher achievers and their parents were more satisfied with family relations, that the boys had greater motivation to please their parents, and that they more often described their parents as thoughtful, understanding, and interested in them.

On the elementary school level, Drews and Teahan studied groups of students who were comparable on aptitude but not on academic performance.[73] They found that the mothers of the higher-achieving students tended to be dominating as well as ignoring. The degree of maternal possessiveness was unrelated to high and low performance levels.

Fliegler found that four home patterns predominate in the case of the gifted, low-achieving child: (1) a neutral or uninterested view of education by the parents; (2) overanxious, oversolicitous, easy-going, or inconsistent parental behavior; (3) lukewarm, indifferent parents; (4) lack of a cooperative spirit in the family.[74] He stated that these patterns lead to distrust of people, a negative attitude toward the learning situation, and a lowered level of aspiration.

Summary and Evaluation. While the findings are not consist-ent, it seems clear that family life is an important factor in school achievement. The general picture that seems to emerge is that the student who does well in school comes from a family which has a relatively small number of children, in which the parents exhibit warmth and interest, where the child has a relatively high degree of power in decision-making, and where the family is able to arrive with relative ease at consensus regarding important values and decisions.

Although these studies indicate the importance of the family in relation to academic achievement, they are designed so differently that it is difficult to determine just how comparable they are. Some of them base their conclusions about family life on data gathered from the mother; others concentrate only on the father; and still others are concerned with both parents. Thus, some gen-eralizations about the effects of the "family" are in reality gener-alizations about only very circumscribed aspects of it. Further-more, no systematic attention has been paid to sex differences or to the extent to which findings at one educational level hold for other levels.

Not even touched upon in these studies are questions we have raised earlier concerning the effects on academic performance of differential identification with various reference groups. An ex-ample is the question of what effects the student's differential identification with family and peer groups has in the case where the values of each regarding academic achievement conflict. The answers to such questions await further research.

SUMMARY OF THE STUDIES

This chapter has reviewed studies concerned with the effects of social factors on academic performance. One type of study em-phasizes the effects of ecological and demographic variables. The findings indicate that there are positive relations between socio-economic status and academic performance at all levels except the upper, where the relationships become inverse. The central significance of SES lies in the fact that it summarizes a variety of other factors that are related to academic performance. Sex, religion, geographic region, and urbanism are also related to academic performance. Once again, these variables summarize a variety of underlying characteristics that serve to explain the observed relationships.

Within the sociological tradition of research which emphasizes role relationships in the educational context, investigations of the student-to-student relationship have shown that sociometric measures of acceptability bear some relation to academic performance, although the causal status of the variable is not clear. Work on the influence of informal peer-group norms upon scholarly attainment is a promising area for study.

Research on the student-teacher relationship suggests two generalizations. First, the more the student's attitudes and values coincide with those of the teacher, the higher the student's academic performance will be. Second, characteristics of teacher behavior may affect the performance level of the student.

Studies dealing with the effects of family relationships upon student performance suggest that several characteristics of family life are relevant. The successful student is likely to come from a family where the parents show warmth and interest, where the child has a relatively strong voice in decision-making, and where the family tends to agree regarding the issues it defines as important.

NOTES TO CHAPTER 6

1. Of course it is also possible that in many cases given types of value systems may predispose persons to gravitate into given kinds of life situations.

2. Crowley, Francis J., "The Goals of Male High School Seniors," *Personnel and Guidance Journal*, vol. 37, 1959, pp. 488–492; Friedhoff, W. H., "Relationships Among Various Measures of Socio-economic Status, Social Class Identification, Intelligence, and School Achievement," *Dissertation Abstracts*, vol. 15, 1955, p. 2098; Knief, Lotus M., and James B. Stroud, "Intercorrelations Among Various Intelligence, Achievement, and Social Class Scores," *Journal of Educational Psychology*, vol. 50, 1959, pp. 117–120; Miner, John B., *Intelligence in the United States: A Survey with Conclusions for Manpower Utilization in Education and Employment*, Springer Publishing Co., New York, 1957; Mitchell, James V., Jr., "A Comparison of the Factorial Structure of Cognitive Functions for a High and Low Status Group," *Journal of Educational Psychology*, vol.

47, 1956, pp. 397–414; Noll, Victor H., "Relation of Scores on Davis-Eells Games to Socioeconomic Status, Intelligence Test Results, and School Achievement," *Educational and Psychological Measurement,* vol. 20, 1960, pp. 119–129; Pinneau, Samuel R., and Harold E. Jones, "Development of Mental Abilities," *Review of Educational Research,* vol. 28, 1958, pp. 392–400.

3. Friedhoff, W. H., *op. cit.*

4. Knief, Lotus M., and James B. Stroud, *op. cit.*

5. Rosen, Bernard C., "The Achievement Syndrome: A Psychocultural Dimension of Social Stratification," *American Sociological Review,* vol. 21, 1956, pp. 203–211.

6. *Ibid.*

7. *Ibid.*

8. Strodtbeck, Fred L., "Family Interaction, Values and Achievement," in McClelland, David C., and associates, *Talent and Society,* D. Van Nostrand Co., Inc., Princeton, N.J., 1958, pp. 135–194.

9. Schneider, Louis, and Sverre Lysgaard, "The Deferred Gratification Pattern: A Preliminary Study," *American Sociological Review,* vol. 18, 1953, pp. 142–149.

10. Brim, Orville G., Jr., and Raymond Forer, "A Note on the Relation of Values and Social Structure to Life Planning," *Sociometry,* vol. 19, 1956, pp. 54–60.

11. Crowley, Francis J., *op. cit.,* Hyman, Herbert H., "The Value Systems of Different Classes: A Social Psychological Contribution to the Analysis of Stratification," in Bendix, Reinhard, and Seymour M. Lipset, editors, *Class, Status and Power: A Reader in Social Stratification,* The Free Press, Glencoe, Ill., 1953, pp. 426–442; Sewell, William, Archie O. Haller, and Murray A. Straus, "Social Status and Educational and Occupational Aspiration," *American Sociological Review,* vol. 22, 1957, pp. 67–73; Wilson, Alan B., "Residential Segregation of Social Classes and Aspirations of High School Boys," *American Sociological Review,* vol. 24, 1959, pp. 836–845.

12. Bresee, Clyde W., "Affective Factors Associated with Academic Underachievement in High-School Students," *Dissertation Abstracts,* vol. 17, 1957, pp. 90–91; Coster, John K., "Some Characteristics of High School Pupils from Three Income Groups," *Journal of Educational Psychology,* vol. 50, 1959, pp. 55–62; Friedhoff, W. H., *op. cit.;* Gerritz, Harold G. J., "The Relationship of Certain Personal and Socio-economic Data to the Success of Resident Freshmen Enrolled in the College of Science, Literature and the Arts at the University of Minnesota," *Dissertation Abstracts,* vol. 16, 1956, p. 2366; Gibboney, Richard A., "Socioeconomic Status and Achievement in Social Studies," *Elementary School Journal,* vol. 59, 1959, pp. 340–346; Knief, Lotus M., and James B. Stroud, *op. cit.;* McKnight, A. James, "The Relation of Certain Home Factors to College Achievement," *Dissertation Abstracts,* vol. 19, 1958, pp. 870–871; McQuary, John P., "Some Relationships Between Non-In-

tellectual Characteristics and Academic Achievement," *Journal of Educational Psychology*, vol. 44, 1953, pp. 215–228; Mueller, Kate H., and John H. Mueller, "Class Structure and Academic and Social Success," *Educational and Psychological Measurement*, vol. 13, 1953, pp. 486–496; Noll, Victor H., *op. cit.;* Ratchick, Irving, "Achievement and Capacity: A Comparative Study of Pupils with Low Achievement and High Intelligence Quotients with Pupils of High Achievement and High Intelligence Quotients in a Selected New York City High School," *Dissertation Abstracts,* vol. 13, 1953, pp. 1049–1050; Rosen, Bernard C., *op. cit.;* Travers, Robert M. W., "Significant Research on the Prediction of Academic Success," in Donahue, W. T., C. H. Coombs, and R. M. W. Travers, editors, *The Measurement of Student Adjustment and Achievement*, University of Michigan Press, Ann Arbor, 1949.

13. Boyce, E. M., "A Comparative Study of Overachieving and Underachieving College Students on Factors Other Than Scholastic Aptitude," *Dissertation Abstracts,* vol. 16, 1956, pp. 2088–2089; Davis, Junius A., "Differential College Achievement of Public vs. Private School Graduates," *Journal of Counseling Psychology,* vol. 3, 1956, pp. 72–73; Davis, Junius A., and Norman Frederiksen, "Public and Private School Graduates in College," *Journal of Teacher Education,* vol. 6, 1955, pp. 18–22; McArthur, Charles C., "Personalities of Public and Private School Boys," *Harvard Educational Review,* vol. 24, 1954, pp. 256–262; McArthur, Charles C., "Subculture and Personality During the College Years," *Journal of Educational Sociology,* vol. 33, 1960, pp. 260–268; Shuey, Audrey M., "Academic Success of Public and Private School Students in Randolph Macon Women's College: I. The Freshman Year," *Journal of Educational Research,* vol. 49, 1956, pp. 481–492.

14. Davis, Junius A., *op. cit.;* Davis, Junius A., and Norman Frederiksen, *op. cit.;* McArthur, Charles C., "Personalities of Public and Private School Boys . . . ," *op. cit.;* McArthur, Charles C., "Subculture and Personality . . . , *op. cit.*

15. Davis, Junius A., *op. cit.;* Davis, Junius A., and Norman Frederiksen, *op. cit.*

16. McArthur, Charles C., "Personalities of Public and Private School Boys . . . ," *op. cit.*

17. *Ibid.;* McArthur, Charles C., "Subculture and Personality . . . ," *op. cit.*

18. Davidson, Helen H., and Gerhard Lang, "Children's Perceptions of Their Teachers' Feelings Toward Them Related to Self-Perception, School Achievement and Behavior," *Journal of Experimental Education,* vol. 29, 1960, pp. 107–118.

19. Gerritz, Harold G. J., *op. cit.;* Hoyt, Donald P., "Size of High School and College Grades," *Personnel and Guidance Journal,* vol. 37, 1959, pp. 569–573; Hughes, Mildred C., "Sex Differences in Reading Achievement in the Elementary Grades," *Supplementary Educational Monographs,* no. 77, 1953, pp. 102–106; Jackson, Robert A., "Prediction

of the Academic Success of College Freshmen," *Journal of Educational Psychology,* vol. 46, 1955, pp. 296–301; Northby, Arwood S., "Sex Differences in High-School Scholarship," *School and Society,* vol. 86, 1958, pp. 63–64; Shaw, Merville C., and John T. McCuen, "The Onset of Academic Underachievement in Bright Children," *Journal of Educational Psychology,* vol. 51, 1960, pp. 103–108.

20. Hughes, Mildred C., *op. cit.*

21. Shaw, Merville C., and John T. McCuen, *op. cit.*

22. This method of defining underachievement does not meet the criteria discussed in Chapter 2. It would be more accurate simply to state that within a sample of students comparable as to ability, there are significant differences in level of academic performance.

23. Parsons, Talcott, "Certain Primary Sources and Patterns of Aggression in the Social Structure of the Western World," in Patrick Mullahy, editor, *A Study of Interpersonal Relations.* Hermitage House, New York, 1949, pp. 284–287.

24. If, as we have stated earlier, the academic performance of females is more predictable than that of males when intellective factors are used as the predictors, then it follows that over- and underachievement should be more frequent for the males.

25. Strodtbeck, Fred L., *op. cit.*

26. Gerritz, Harold G. J., *op. cit.*

27. Rossi, Peter H., "Social Factors in Academic Achievement: A Brief Review," in Halsey, A. H., Jean Floud, and C. A. Anderson, editors, *Education, Economy, and Society,* The Free Press, New York, 1961, pp. 269–272.

28. Shaw, Merville C., and Donald J. Brown, "Scholastic Underachievement of Bright College Students," *Personnel and Guidance Journal,* vol. 36, 1957, pp. 195–199; Washburne, Norman F., "Socioeconomic Status, Urbanism and Academic Performance in College," *Journal of Educational Research,* vol. 53, 1959, pp. 130–137.

29. Sanders, William B., R. Travis Osborne, and Joel E. Greene, "Intelligence and Academic Performance of College Students of Urban, Rural, and Mixed Backgrounds," *Journal of Educational Research,* vol. 49, 1955, pp. 185–193.

30. Carter, Lowell, "The Effect of Early School Entrance on the Scholastic Achievement of Elementary School Children in the Austin Public Schools," *Journal of Educational Research,* vol. 50, 1956, pp. 91–103.

31. Stephany, Edward Oscar, "Academic Achievement in Grades Five Through Nine," *Dissertation Abstracts,* vol. 16, 1956, p. 1846.

32. Miller, Vera V., "Academic Achievement and Social Adjustment of Children Young for Their Grade Placement," *Elementary School Journal,* vol. 57, 1957, pp. 257–263.

33. Hoyt, Donald P., *op. cit.*

34. Altman, Esther R., "The Effect of Rank in Class and Size of High School on the Academic Achievement of Central Michigan College Seniors, Class of 1957," *Journal of Educational Research*, vol. 52, 1959, pp. 307–309.

35. Andrew, Dean C., "Relationship Between Academic Load and Scholastic Success of Deficient Students," *Personnel and Guidance Journal*, vol. 34, 1956, pp. 268–270; Hountras, Peter Timothy, "The Relationship Between Student Load and Achievement," *Journal of Educational Research*, vol. 51, 1958, pp. 355–360; Merrill, Reed M., and Hal W. Osborn, "Academic Overload and Scholastic Success," *Personnel and Guidance Journal*, vol. 37, 1959, pp. 509–510; Schwilk, Gene L., "Academic Achievement of Freshmen High School Students in Relationship to Class Load and Scholastic Aptitude," *Personnel and Guidance Journal*, vol. 37, 1959, pp. 455–456; Shaw, Merville C., and Donald J. Brown, *op. cit.*

36. Johnson, Edward E., "Student Ratings of Popularity and Scholastic Ability of Their Peers and Actual Scholastic Performance of Those Peers," *Journal of Social Psychology*, vol. 47, 1958, pp. 127–132.

37. Zumwinkle, Robert G., "Factors Associated with the Compatability of Roommates: A Test of the Birds of a Feather Hypothesis," *Dissertation Abstracts*, vol. 14, 1954, p. 563.

38. Edminston, R. W., and Betty Jane Rhoades, "Predicting Achievement," *Journal of Educational Research*, vol. 52, 1959, pp. 177–180.

39. Ryan, F. R., and James S. Davie, "Social Acceptance, Academic Achievement, and Aptitude Among High School Students," *Journal of Educational Research*, vol. 52, 1958, pp. 101–106.

40. Keisler, Evan R., "Peer Group Rating of High School Pupils with High and Low School Marks," *Journal of Experimental Education*, vol. 23, 1955, pp. 375–378.

41. Coleman, James S., "Academic Achievement and the Structure of Competition," *Harvard Educational Review*, vol. 29, 1959, pp. 330–351; Coleman, James S., *The Adolescent Society*, The Free Press, New York, 1961.

42. Homans, George C., *The Human Group*. Harcourt, Brace and Co., New York, 1950.

43. Buswell, M., "Relationship Between the Social Structure of the Classroom and the Academic Success of the Pupils," *Journal of Experimental Education*, vol. 22, 1953, pp. 37–52; Lloyd R. Grann, and associates, "The Relationship Between Academic Achievement of Pupils and the Social Structure of the Classroom," *Rural Sociology*, vol. 21, 1956, pp. 179–180.

44. Quay, Lorene, "Academic Achievement Attitudes in Group Perception in Sixth Graders," *Dissertation Abstracts*, vol. 19, 1959, pp. 3042–3043.

45. Yourglich, Anita, "Study on Correlations Between College Teach-

ers' and Students' Concepts of 'Ideal-Student' and 'Ideal-Teacher,' " *Journal of Educational Research*, vol. 49, 1955, pp. 59–64.

46. Kelly, Eldon G., "A Study of Consistent Discrepancies Between Instructor Grades and Term-End Examination Grades," *Journal of Educational Psychology*, vol. 49, 1958, pp. 328–334.

47. Battle, Haron J., "Relation Between Personal Values and Scholastic Achievement," *Journal of Experimental Education*, vol. 26, 1957, pp. 27–41.

48. Carter, Robert S., "Non-Intellectual Variables Involved in Teachers' Marks," *Journal of Educational Research*, vol. 47, 1953, pp. 81–95.

49. Siegel, Laurence, and associates, "Expressed Standards of Behavior of High School Students, Teachers, and Parents," *Personnel and Guidance Journal*, vol. 34, 1956, pp. 261–267.

50. Moss, Howard, "Standards of Conduct for Students, Teachers, and Parents," *Journal of Counseling Psychology*, vol. 2, 1955, pp. 39–42.

51. Getzels, Jacob W., and Philip W. Jackson, "Family Environment and Cognitive Style: A Study of the Sources of Highly Intelligent and of Highly Creative Adolescents," *American Sociological Review*, vol. 26, 1961, pp. 351–359; a more detailed report of this study is available in a volume by the same authors, *Creativity and Intelligence:* Explorations with Gifted Students, John Wiley and Sons, New York, 1962. In a review of this volume, Cronbach points out that these two groups may not be very different in true IQ, and this may account for the fact that they are similar in achievement (in *The American Journal of Sociology*, vol. 68, 1962, pp. 278–279).

52. Malpass, Leslie F., "Some Relationships Between Students' Perceptions of School and Their Achievement," *Journal of Educational Psychology*, vol. 44, 1953, pp. 475–482.

53. Davidson, Helen H., and Gerhard Lang, *op. cit.*

54. It should be noted that intelligence was not controlled in this study. Thus, perceived favorableness might be simply an indirect index of ability.

55. Baker, Robert L., and Roy P. Doyle, "Teacher Knowledge of Pupil Data and Marking Practices at the Elementary School Level," *Personnel and Guidance Journal*, vol. 37, 1959, pp. 644–647.

56. Ryans, David G., "Some Relationships Between Pupil Behavior and Certain Teacher Characteristics," *Journal of Educational Psychology*, vol. 52, 1961, pp. 82–90; Ryans, David G., *Characteristics of Teachers: Their Description, Comparison, and Appraisal,* American Council on Education, Washington, D.C., 1960.

57. Rosenfeld, Howard M., and Alvin Zander, "The Influence of Teachers on Aspirations of Students," *Journal of Educational Psychology*, vol. 52, 1961, pp. 1–11.

58. Christensen, Clifford M., "Relationships Between Pupil Achieve-

ment, Pupil Affect-Need, Teacher Warmth, and Teacher Permissiveness," *Journal of Educational Psychology,* vol. 51, 1960, pp. 169–174.

59. Stringer, Lorene A., "Academic Progress as an Index of Mental Health," *The Journal of Social Issues,* vol. 15, 1959, pp. 16–29.

60. Newcomb, Theodore M., *Personality and Social Change.* Dryden Press, New York, 1943.

61. Bernstein, B., "Some Sociological Determinants of Perception; An Enquiry into Sub-Cultural Differences," *British Journal of Sociology,* vol. 9, 1958, pp. 159–174.

62. Nisbet, J., "Family Environment and Intelligence," in Halsey, A. H., Jean Floud, and Charles A. Anderson, editors, *op. cit.* pp. 273–287.

63. Hunt, Joseph McVicker, *Intelligence and Experience.* The Ronald Press, New York, 1961.

64. Bernstein, B., "Social Class and Linguistic Development: A Theory of Social Learning," in Halsey, A. H., Jean Floud, and Charles A. Anderson, *op. cit.,* pp. 288–314.

65. Weitz, Henry J., and H. Jean Wilkinson, "The Relationship Between Certain Non-intellective Factors and Academic Success in College," *Journal of Counseling Psychology,* vol. 4, 1957, pp. 54–60.

66. Nisbet, J., *op. cit.*

67. Schoonover, Sarah M., "The Relationship of Intelligence and Achievement to Birth Order, Sex of Sibling, and Age Interval," *Journal of Educational Psychology,* vol. 50, 1959, pp. 143–146.

68. Brim, Orville G., Jr., "Family Structure and Sex Role Learning by Children: A Further Analysis of Helen Koch's Data," *Sociometry,* vol. 21, 1958, pp. 1–15.

69. Strodtbeck, Fred L., *op. cit.*

70. Gilmore, John V., "A New Venture in the Testing of Motivation," *College Board Review,* vol. 15, 1951, pp. 221–226.

71. Kimball, Barbara, "Case Studies in Educational Failure During Adolescence," *American Journal of Orthopsychiatry,* vol. 23, 1953, pp. 406–415.

72. Tibbetts, John R., "The Role of Parent-Child Relationships in the Achievement of High School Pupils: A Study of the Family Relationships Associated with Underachievement and High Achievement of High School Pupils," *Dissertation Abstracts,* vol. 15, 1955, p. 232.

73. Drews, Elizabeth, and John E. Teahan, "Parental Attitudes and Academic Achievement," *Journal of Clinical Psychology,* vol. 13, 1957, pp. 328–332.

74. Fliegler, Louis A., "Understanding the Underachieving Gifted Child," *Psychological Reports,* vol. 3, 1957, pp. 533–536.

Chapter 7

Directions for Future Research: The Social Structure and Personality Approach

IT IS A TRUISM in behavioral science that behavior is a function of personality and situational characteristics. In one form or another this idea finds expression in most current theories of behavior. Yet little of the research reviewed thus far has considered both aspects of this proposition. In Chapter 5 we saw that the psychologist looks for the effects of personality factors that cut across variations in social environments, and Chapter 6 illustrated how the sociologist investigates the characteristics of social environments that transcend individual personalities. In other words, in their "pure" forms, both the psychological and sociological traditions attempt to examine the main effects of each type of variable on academic performance.

Recently signs have emerged that indicate a developing research effort devoted to the assessment of both personality and situational characteristics. It emphasizes the ways in which individual differences in personality interact with characteristics of the social environment to affect academic performance. Thus, certain personality characteristics may lead to high achievement in some social settings but not in others, and some kinds of social environments may be conducive to high achievement for certain types of personalities but not for others.

This last chapter begins with a review of studies of this type. Because we feel the approach is most promising and in need of further development, the chapter continues with a discussion of

157

some of the directions which future research might take. In this connection an illustrative research design is presented. Finally, we conclude with some general remarks about the state of knowledge regarding academic achievement.

THE FINDINGS

The investigations cited in this section deal with the measurement of characteristics of personality and of social environments. Not all of them are directly concerned with the prediction of academic performance. Nevertheless, we review them because they could be applied to this problem.

Research by Stern, Stein, and Bloom, cited in Chapter 5, suggested that college students with particular personality characteristics performed better in some curricular areas than in others because the areas were hospitable to particular personality types but not to others.[1] This investigation led to the development of a research program by Stern, Pace, and their associates, aimed at assessing the relations between students' personalities and school environments.[2] The approach involves two types of measures: one examines the structure of personality needs; the second type assesses the characteristics of the college environment. The dimensions used for characterizing both the personality and the environment derive from a conceptual framework made up of a series of coordinated concepts drawn from Murray's need-press schema.[3] Personality is measured as a series of needs, and the environment is viewed as a series of "presses." For example, the personality measure contains a scale assessing the need for order, and the measure of environmental characteristics contains a parallel scale assessing the degree to which there are pressures upon students to be orderly. In other words, the term "press" refers to those aspects of the environment that tend to satisfy or deprive an individual characterized by a given need. Evidence indicates that even though the same subjects provide the relevant information on needs and presses, the two are independent of each other.[4]

While this approach has not been used to predict academic performance, one can immediately see its potentialities for this question. For example, congruence profiles between needs and presses can readily be computed. Thus, for some students there will be a rather close "fit" between their needs and school presses, and for others there will be a relative lack of fit. The lack of congruence for the latter students might lower their academic motivation.

One study drawing partly from the work of Stern and associates was conducted by Thistlethwaite.[5] He was interested in assessing the relation between college environments and achievement. He defined achievement as the proportion of alumni who earned a Ph.D. degree. Using a sample of National Merit Scholars distributed among 36 colleges, he administered the Pace and Stern College Characteristics Index (the press measure). On the assumption that these subjects' responses were valid for ten to fifteen years earlier at each college, the productivity of each institution was divided into two categories: (1) the number of Ph.D.'s in natural science and (2) the number of Ph.D.'s in the arts, humanities, and social sciences (AHSS). Measures of press were then divided according to whether they referred to student press (peer group norms) or faculty press (faculty demands). It was found that college press encouraging science productivity is different from that promoting AHSS productivity. Colleges with high AHSS productivity exhibit a student climate characterized by humanism, breadth of interest, reflectiveness, low participation in mass social activities, and low aggression. Faculty press at such colleges is characterized by such factors as energy and controversy in instruction, informal faculty-student contact, and flexibility of curriculum. On the other hand, colleges high in science productivity are characterized by student press which is high on aggression and scientism, and low on social conformity. Faculty press at these colleges exhibits characteristics such as low directiveness of teaching methods and lack of close faculty supervision. This study does not fully utilize the work of Stern and his associates, since no attempt has been made to assess personality patterns within the various colleges.

A scattering of other studies focus on both personality and socioenvironmental factors. One interesting study of a sample of college women was carried out by Applezweig and associates.[6] An attempt was made to predict academic performance through the use of two motivational characteristics: need for achievement and need for affiliation. It was hypothesized that these are mutually reinforcing or mutually conflicting, depending upon the achievement norms of a student's particular friendship clique. For example, a subject who is low on need for achievement but high on need for affiliation will be expected to do better scholastically if his friendship group places a high value on academic achievement than if it places a lower value on academic achievement. In short, there is a general hypothesis that properties of the social environment (in this case peer group norms regarding achievement) will interact with specific personality needs so as to increase or decrease the student's level of academic performance. In this study the measure of need for affiliation proved to be inadequate, and the working assumption was made that this need was equal for all subjects. The data suggest that subjects high on need for achievement who are members of cliques that are high on this motive do better in school than subjects who have high achievement motivation but who are members of cliques that are low on this need. In addition, subjects who are low on need for achievement but who belong to groups that are high on need for achievement do better than subjects who are low on the need and who belong to groups that are low on achievement motivation. While these findings are only suggestive and the research may be criticized for failure to control adequately for intelligence, the study well illustrates how both social and psychological factors may be used for the prediction of academic performance.

Beach conducted another study that takes into account both personality and situational factors.[7] He studied the relationship between sociability and academic achievement in four different kinds of learning situations—a lecture class, a discussion group with instructor, a leaderless discussion group, and an independent study group. Students low on sociability performed better in the lecture section and in instructor-led groups, and the more sociable students performed better in the leaderless discussion groups. Thus, this research suggests that sociability takes on meaning as a personality characteristic when it is viewed within the context of the social climate of the classroom. That is, students with high sociability perform better in class situations in which interaction is more frequent (discussion groups), while students who are not sociable perform better in situations in which interaction is at a minimum (the lecture class).

SUMMARY AND EVALUATION

The studies discussed above certainly do not provide any definitive statements about the effects on academic performance of the interactions between personality and socioenvironmental factors. However, they do suggest that more research along these lines may prove useful. In particular, the personality and social structure approach may help to clarify a question that arose in Chapter 5; namely, why have certain personality characteristics been found to be good predictors at some schools but not at others? We can now see that variability in the predictive usefulness of personality variables may in part be attributed to the different social contexts in which they are used.

Even though little research of this type has been carried out, certain limitations, especially in the approach of Stern and his associates, are already apparent. In particular, the need-press conception oversimplifies the social environment. For example, when the degree of achievement press at a college is measured, there is a mixture of items, some referring to perceptions of faculty expectations, others referring to student norms. That is, institutional characteristics are described on the most general basis rather than in terms of specific role systems. To characterize the social context in such gross terms disregards the possibility that the press in one role system may not be similar to the press in another. For example, it may be that on various dimensions the faculty press conflicts with the press of the student peer culture. Such inconsistency could have effects on academic performance quite different from that of a consistent situation. The conception of the social environment developed by Stern and colleagues is too broad to allow one to study questions such as this.

These questions can be considered through a more specific approach, however, as exemplified in the work of sociologists such as Neal Gross and associates on role theory.[8] These investigators stress the need to look at social positions in terms of the different counter-positions to which they are related in the educational system. Thus, there is the relation of student to student, of student to teacher, and of student to college administrative officials. These counter-positions may define different and possibly conflicting expectations for the student role. The effect of such conflict upon the academic performance of students with different personality characteristics should be assessed. Even within the student-to-student relational system there may be different cliques, each with its own particular value system, and the position of a given student vis-à-vis all of these may affect his level of achievement.

Another issue is that the need-press approach, by definition, "psychologizes" social structure. That is, the dimensions characterizing the social environment are derived from and coordinated with concepts originally formulated for the description of personality. While sociologists may object to this, to some extent the issue is semantic, and the usefulness of the Stern approach will have to be evaluated on pragmatic grounds. As in any area of research, however, it is desirable that alternative formulations be developed and tested.[9]

AN ILLUSTRATIVE STUDY DESIGN FOR FUTURE RESEARCH

While Chapter 5 shows that personality characteristics can affect achievement level, and Chapter 6, that there are social environments that are more or less conducive to the attainment of high achievement levels, neither approach has been strikingly successful. This does not necessarily mean that the variables studied are not useful. Rather we think that the *strategy* of research is at fault; that is, neither psychological nor sociological factors alone are capable of substantially enhancing our understanding of academic achievement. We propose that it is at the level of the interaction between these two types of factors that any major breakthrough is likely to come, and for this reason we believe that the personality and social structure approach holds the most promise, even though no solid body of research yet exists. Since this is the case, we wish now to sketch out a concrete research design as an example of what might be done. What follows is intended to serve as an illustration of one alternative, rather than as a definitive model.

Attention will focus upon three variables: need for affiliation, need for achievement, and peer group value systems.[10] The first two are personality variables; the third is a sociological characteristic.

Need for affiliation is defined as the desire to form and maintain social relationships. Students high on this need are expected to exhibit higher rates of interaction with their peers than students who are low on this need. Furthermore, because deviation from group norms may threaten the maintenance of social relationships, we assume that the person with strong affiliative needs will be more likely to yield to group pressures than the person who is less affiliative. This factor should be measured in several ways, such as through self-reports about desires for sociability and through self and peer ratings on frequency of interaction.

Need for achievement is defined as the desire to perform according to a high standard of excellence—in this case academic excellence. Techniques and problems in the measurement of this variable have been discussed in Chapter 5. Suffice it to say that it should be measured on different levels (on both a general and a more specific level involving academic motivation) and by objective as well as projective methods.

The assessment of peer group value systems requires a number of procedures. First, it is necessary to map out the clique structure within a school through sociometric techniques. The value system of each clique then could be determined by asking the members to choose among a variety of paired activities, each of which expresses a particular value. For example, members could be asked whether their group would usually choose going to a movie over attending a guest lecture or a concert. From such questions the value priorities of the clique could be defined. Thus, in some cliques activities of a scholarly and intellectual nature might rank very high, and in others they might rank low.

Having measured each of these variables, various types of interactions between them could be used for the prediction of academic performance levels. These interactions are presented in Chart 3. Thus, cell A refers to a student who is high on need for affiliation and on need for achievement, and who belongs to a peer subgroup that places a high value on academic excellence. Cell E, on the other hand, represents a student who is similar to the one in cell A with regard to personality but is a member of a student peer group that places a relatively low value upon academic performance.

The variations presented in Chart 3 have implications for academic performance levels.[11] We would expect that students in cell A would exhibit a higher level of academic performance than students in cell E. We would predict this because the student in cell E is likely to find that his need for acceptance in a group that does not highly value scholarly activity may detract from his academic effort. We would also expect that the student falling in cell B would exhibit a higher level of performance than the student falling in cell F. In both cases, achievement motivation is low. However, in cell B the student's high need for affiliation may impel him toward greater effort because of the demands of his peer group, which define scholarly activity as important. Thus,

CHART 3.   INTERACTIONS BETWEEN NEED FOR AFFILIATION, NEED FOR ACHIEVEMENT, AND PEER GROUP VALUE SYSTEM

Peer group value system regarding academic excellence	Need for affiliation			
	High		Low	
	Need for achievement		Need for achievement	
	High	Low	High	Low
Excellence highly valued	(A)	(B)	(C)	(D)
Excellence not highly valued	(E)	(F)	(G)	(H)

in order to maintain acceptance in the group, the student may work harder. On the other hand, in cell F the student's low achievement motivation is paralleled by a low degree of emphasis upon scholarship in his peer group. We would therefore expect the performance of this student to fall below the level of his counterpart in cell B.

We might also compare all students in cells A, B, E, and F with students in cells C, D, G, and H. We would predict that for the former, the effect of the peer group norms will be more important than for the latter. Since the latter are low on need for affiliation, this implies that they will be less sensitive to group pressures. Consequently, for these students achievement motivation will tend to operate independently of the peer group value system. To put it another way, we would expect that for this group of students, need for achievement will be a more efficient single predictor of academic performance than for students having high need for affiliation. In short, being low on need for affiliation would tend to "wash out" the effects of peer group pressures. Therefore, if the student in cell C is compared with the student in cell G, the differences between them (in academic performance) should be smaller than the differences observed when the student in cell A is compared with the one in cell E.

We suggest that the approach outlined above will contribute more to our understanding of academic performance than either the psychological approach described in Chapter 5 or the sociological approach presented in Chapter 6. Academic achievement is determined by complex interactions of predictor variables; therefore, we need models that attempt to approximate this complexity. The model described here seems to come closer to this ideal than either of the separate approaches. However, the empirical situation is undoubtedly much more complex than portrayed above. In the first place, we have assumed that there is only one significant subgroup to which a student belongs. However, as noted earlier, all students have multiple-group membership within just the school situation alone. Thus, we must consider the degree to which the student's membership groups present him with conflicting as against mutually supporting or converging value systems. The degree of conflict resulting from multiple-group membership may be a variable having important implications for student academic performance.

Furthermore, cliques may vary not only in terms of value priorities, but also in terms of the pressures they exert for conformity to these values. If we take two peer group cliques both of which place great emphasis upon intellectual pursuits, one may permit considerably more deviation from its standards than the other. Therefore, this factor itself may accentuate or decrease the effect of group norms upon performance.

We have dealt here with only two personality variables and only one role system (the student-to-student relationship). The whole approach becomes even more complex when one considers the total range of relevant personality variables as well as the range of relevant environmental characteristics. Significant advances in the understanding of academic achievement should be made when social-psychological research comes to grips with considerations of this type.

CONCLUDING REMARKS

It would be appropriate at the conclusion of this volume to discuss the implications of research for those who, in their professional educational roles, are most likely to need such information. Clearly, personnel such as college admissions officers, high school guidance counselors, deans, and teachers must, to varying degrees, either make decisions or help others make decisions that will significantly affect the course of students' lives. However, the state of knowledge in this field is not yet at a sufficiently definitive level to be used confidently for such practical decision-making. This statement applies particularly to the research on personality and socioenvironmental factors. In these areas too little is presently known to allow practical application. Of course, ability measures do play a large role in current educational decision-making. However, this kind of information is certainly not sufficient in itself. If it were, there would be no need for additional research dealing with nonintellective factors. Thus, a discussion of implications for practice must remain a goal to be achieved rather than an accomplished end.

While the body of research reviewed and evaluated in this volume may present a rather disappointing picture from the practical point of view, there are many encouraging signs, and we have attempted to highlight these at various points. However, further development of currently suggestive research areas will require a broader approach than usually has been exhibited.

One source of difficulty is that this research area is strongly defined as an applied field, and applied fields have a way of becoming divorced from more fundamental concerns. But it should be clear from several earlier remarks that understanding the determinants of academic achievement involves fundamental theoretical questions. This is true in two senses. On the one hand, researchers in this field must make greater use of basic findings, even though these findings may not have emerged originally from research on educational performance. On the other hand, there is no question that research on academic achievement can make significant contributions to fundamental knowledge of behavior. Those who define themselves as educational psychologists or as educational sociologists should broaden their horizons. For those whose concerns are the development and evaluation of basic theory, the study of academic performance provides a rich testing ground.

The result of such cross-fertilization should be a more accurate model for predicting academic performance. It has been a major purpose of this volume to point out the directions in which we should move if a better model is to be developed.

But assuming for a moment that we had such a model, what should be done with it? How should it be applied? For the sake of discussion, let us assume that we are able to predict academic performance with 100 per cent accuracy. And suppose, for example, our model indicated that at a certain college students with a given set of personality characteristics always achieved at a higher scholastic level than students with some other set of personality characteristics, other things being equal. Should such information be used by admissions offices to exclude the latter type from entrance? We think not. In the first place, as pointed out in Chapter 1, there is little evidence that school grades alone are closely related to any significant criteria lying beyond the completion of the educational career. For this reason, we need to develop additional dimensions of student performance and to find out how they relate to various aspects of life after the completion of school. If such dimensions are discovered, and if good performance on them is predictable, then the predictive characteristics could be justified as bases for admission to college. But to look mainly for students whose academic performance will be high without considering the reasons for our interest in high performance may, in the long run, be unfair to society as well as to the excluded students. Many of our most distinguished citizens who attended famous universities had college and graduate school careers that were hardly outstanding, even though their educational experiences may have benefited them in some unknown but important ways not measured by their grade-point average. If they were to begin over again, many of them would be unable to qualify for admission to their distinguished alma maters.

In sum, research on the prediction of academic performance needs to be expanded, not just in terms of developing better predictive models, but also in terms of discovering more meaningful sets of performance criteria (that is, criteria related to "significant" aspects of life after completion of school). Certain types of personalities may not, for various reasons, compile outstanding academic records, but they might nevertheless be suited for outstanding contributions later on, and what they gain from education is not necessarily measured by their school grades. If we can conceptualize, and can measure new dimensions of student performance, and if performance can be predicted accurately, such knowledge could be used in admissions.

However, admissions decisions are not the only use to which predictive models can be put. They can also be used for modifying educational organizations so that schools can achieve their purposes more readily. For example, assuming that one goal of liberal education at most colleges is to develop in its students an enduring commitment to intellectual inquiry—that is, an interest in ideas for their own sake and the development of qualities of critical-mindedness—in what ways can educational institutions create conditions conducive to their development? It would require another book to explore them all. However, a partial answer would involve the consideration of student subcultures. We have seen in Chapter 6 that these subcultures have important effects on academic performance because they create strong pressures for adherence to their norms. Where the norms are anti-intellectual or nonintellectual and are instead "fun-" or play-oriented, many students may be prevented from working as close to their level of aptitude as otherwise they might, and, more important in the present context, they may develop poor attitudes toward intellectual activity. Moreover, students are differentially sensitive to peer group standards. The students most susceptible to peer pressures of this sort may become seriously incapacitated in their attitudes toward learning. Of course, students who are not susceptible may develop a high level of intellectual commitment while paying a heavy price in other satisfactions.

Conceivably we may be able to exercise some control over the problems created by the student subcultures that work against a school's purposes. We need research on at least three questions. First, how do sociometric groupings of students form; that is, can we predict which students will become friends?[12] Second, why do particular subcultures develop the norms they do?[13] And third, can the normative content be changed—especially where the norms tend to downgrade intellectual endeavor? While little is currently known about these questions, some of the directions for application are clear. Thus, if we knew the conditions leading certain individuals to form a clique and could predict the kinds of norms the group will develop, some control might be obtained—for example, through roommate assignments in the freshman year of college.

Clearly, a model which could predict student performance with great power would have to have built into it some conception of the operation and formation of student subcultures. That is, it would have to contain answers to why cliques form and why they develop a particular set of values. Such a model might be used to furnish leads as to how to modify the content of student sub-cultures so as to encourage intellectual commitment. This use implies the necessity of a different view of the school on the part of the educator. Currently, the dominant view at most schools is a passive one; that is, students are selected because it is expected that they can do well at the school. Thus, the school organization is viewed as static; it is the student who must fit in with it. How-ever, what we are advocating is the notion that many of the qual-ities which schools hope to inculcate in students are dependent on certain organizational characteristics of the school and that modifications in the organization are capable of developing these qualities to varying degrees.

In short, a greatly broadened context is needed. In terms of the criteria to be predicted, we need dimensions of performance whose relation to life after the completion of school is established. Practically, predictive models can be useful not only for the tra-ditional tasks such as admissions, but also as a basis for modifying organizational structure, thus aiding in the attainment of educa-tional goals.

NOTES TO CHAPTER 7

1. Stern, George G., Morris I. Stein, and Benjamin S. Bloom, *Methods in Personality Assessment*. The Free Press, Glencoe, Ill., 1956.

2. Illustrative of this work are the following: Pace, C. Robert, and George G. Stern, "An Approach to the Measurement of Psychological Characteristics of College Environments," *Journal of Educational Psy-chology*, vol. 49, 1958, pp. 269–277; Pace, C. Robert, "Five College Envi-ronments," *College Board Review*, vol. 42, 1960, pp. 24–28; Stern, George G., "Congruence and Dissonance in the Ecology of College Students," *Student Medicine*, vol. 8, 1960, pp. 304–339; Stern, George G., "Student Values and Their Relationship to the College Environment," in Sprague, H. T., editor, *Research on College Students*, Western Commission for Higher Education, Boulder, Colo., 1960, pp. 67–104; Stern, George G., "The Measurement of Psychological Characteristics of Students and Learn-ing Environments," in Messick, S. J., and J. Ross, editors, *Measurement in Personality and Cognition*, John Wiley and Sons, New York, 1962, pp. 27–68.

3. For a description of Murray's system, see Hall, Calvin S., and Gard-ner Lindzey, *Theories of Personality*, John Wiley and Sons, New York, 1957, chap. 5.

4. McFee, Anne, "The Relation of Students' Needs to Their Perceptions of a College Environment," *Journal of Educational Psychology,* vol. 1, 1961, pp. 25–29.

5. Thistlethwaite, Donald L., "College Press and Student Achievement," *Journal of Educational Psychology,* vol. 50, 1959, pp. 183–191.

6. Applezweig, Mortimer H., George Moeller, and Harvey Burdick, "Multi-Motive Prediction of Academic Success," *Psychological Reports,* vol. 2, 1956, pp. 489–496.

7. Beach, Leslie R., "Sociability and Academic Achievement in Various Types of Learning Situations," *Journal of Educational Psychology,* vol. 51, 1960, pp. 208–212.

8. Gross, Neal, Ward S. Mason, and Alexander W. McEachern, *Explorations in Role Analysis.* John Wiley and Sons, New York, 1958.

9. For an alternative formulation of dimensions for the analysis of educational organizations, see the recent monograph by Allen H. Barton, *Organizational Measurement and Its Bearing on the Study of College Environments,* College Entrance Examination Board, New York, 1961.

10. The ensuing discussion derives in part from the report of Mortimer H. Applezweig, George G. Moeller, and Harvey Burdick, *op. cit.*

11. This discussion assumes, of course, that ability factors are controlled.

12. A recent study on this topic is reported in Newcomb, Theodore M., *The Acquaintance Process,* Holt, Rinehart and Winston, New York, 1961.

13. An attempt to develop a theoretical approach for the explanation of normative content is presented in Cohen, Albert K., *Delinquent Boys,* The Free Press, Glencoe, Ill., 1955.

Index

Index